C000016275

*Successful
public
relations*

Successful public relations

The insider's way to get
successful media coverage

JIM DUNN

© 1988, 1993 Hawksmere plc

Published by:
Hawksmere plc
12–18 Grosvenor Gardens
Belgravia
London
SW1 0DH

ISBN 1 85418 031 2

A CIP catalogue record for this book is available from the
British Library.

All rights reserved. No part of this publication may be reproduced, stored in a retrieval system, or transmitted, in any form
or by any means, electronic, mechanical, photocopying, recording or otherwise, without either the prior written permission of
the copyright holder for which application should be addressed
in the first instance to the publishers or a licence permitting
restricted copying issued by the Copyright Licensing Agency
Ltd, 90 Tottenham Court Road, London W1P 9HE.

Design, editorial and production in association with
Book Production Consultants, Cambridge.

Typeset by KeyStar, St Ives, Cambridgeshire

Printed by The Alden Press, Osney Mead, Oxford

To ARTHUR

Acknowledgements

My thanks particularly to my colleague Sarah Wallace for putting up with me throughout this project. Also grateful thanks to the many contributors whose advice and expertise have been invaluable.

JIM DUNN

At 47, Jim Dunn has had almost 25 years in public relations. Following six years in journalism in Britain, he started his own public relations company, TPS Public Relations, in 1969 in the heart of the then British media centre, Fleet Street in London. Jim Dunn is also a director of Hawksmere Limited, the seminar and training group, for whom he regularly gives seminars on public relations.

As a former journalist, he believes strongly that a good public relations practitioner should ideally have a background in newspapers or magazines. 'If this is not the case,' he says, 'anyone coming into public relations should make their first task that of visiting a newspaper, talking to the journalists and finding out how they work and what they require from a public relations person. I'm continually concerned about the lack of understanding of a journalist's job by some public relations people.'

'There is no mystique surrounding good public relations,' he says. 'Good public relations is based on common sense, an alert mind and creativity: of knowing just how much you can accomplish with public relations; accepting that you can't win them all and having the ability to move on to the next exercise when an idea doesn't succeed.'

Jim Dunn enjoyed a very happy period on a Scottish local paper and subsequently in travel trade journalism in London before setting up the TPS Group of public relations companies. He now advises a number of major companies and organisations on PR – both corporately and on their day-to-day contact with the media.

Contents

Appendixes

Introduction

This book is intended to help you, and your company, get the best out of the media through effective public relations. It is certainly not the first-ever book on the subject, but is different in that it has been written mainly by PR practitioners who have also been 'on the other side', working as full-time journalists. The knowledge they have acquired from working on both sides of the fence provides a useful insight into the way the media operates and what it expects from PR practitioners.

The first part of the book contains a step-by-step guide to PR based on the author's experiences, while in the final chapters we look at industry and discuss particular PR requirements and problems, and how they are tackled.

The book sets out to ask, and answer, questions facing everyone involved in PR at whatever level, from chief executives, marketing directors and sales managers of companies large and small to newly appointed public relations officers (PROs) or those who have been in the profession for some time but realise there is still a lot to learn.

- What is PR?

- How can it be used to promote my company, organisation or product?

- Can I make use of PR even with a small budget?

- How do I write an effective press release?

- Do syndicated features work?

- What is 'news' and what isn't?

- How should I deal with the media?

- How do I cope in the event of a disaster or emergency?

These are just some of the many themes tackled in the book, which covers the gamut of PR activities and skills which now, more than ever, are being used by large and small companies, national and multi-national corporations, organisations of all types and sizes, and even political parties, to get their message across.

The reasons that PR has at last 'come of age' are not difficult to understand, because effective use of the media, especially newspapers, magazines and, increasingly, television and radio, can have a dramatic impact on the way a company or organisation and its 'products' – hi-fi equipment, perfume, clothing, motor cars, hotels, airlines or a humble bag of crisps – are not only perceived by the general public, but bought. There are scores of examples of spectacular overnight demand for goods or services as a result of editorial mention in the columns of newspapers and magazines or on television – all resulting from skilful PR techniques. Some examples, with their 'PR costs', are described below.

- A small favourable article in the restaurant column of the *London Standard* resulted in a restaurant being booked out for the best part of three months and certainly put that restaurant on its feet.

PR cost: a meal for two.

- One article in the travel columns (again favourable) resulted in 50 bookings for a package holiday costing around £400 per person.

PR cost: mailing of one *targeted* press release.

- A seven-minute slot on BBC TV looking at a weekend break in a hotel resulted in that particular package being booked out for an entire year and the client gaining an invaluable mailing list of potential customers for future use.

PR cost: two nights' accommodation, some travel expenses and a few meals for a three-person film crew.

- An article in the city pages of the *Sunday Telegraph* on a newly listed company affected – in a positive fashion – the share price.

PR cost: coffee for two.

- A tour by the editor of a new magazine visiting more than 10 local radio stations and giving live interviews resulted in a recognisable sales increase for that magazine in those areas.

PR cost: higher than the other examples because of time input, travelling etc but probably in the region of £1,000.

- A sandpaper manufacturer was successful but needed to increase its profile at the corporate level to industry and that of its individual products to the decision-makers on the shop floor. One phone call to the editor of a trade magazine read by the shop floor resulted in double-page coverage, including a chart setting out a guide to the company's complete abrasive range and which jobs they should be used for. This chart has been reprinted by the company's largest distributor and circulated to 10,000 potential users.

PR cost: overnight accommodation and one lunch (£120).

The list is endless. There are acres of coverage and many, many minutes of airtime available to you and your company through PR.

How did these product 'plugs' get there? Not by themselves, that's for sure, but through the PR professionals being able to interest their media contacts in giving news coverage to particular products.

Good, positive media coverage can generate enormous levels of public interest and increase sales overnight, and more and more companies are now realising that one of the best ways of achieving improved media coverage and exposure is through the use of public relations professionals.

But despite having acquired a much more respectable reputation in recent times, PR activity remains widely misunderstood. For example, it is too often supposed to be just a matter of hunches and lunches and cocktail parties; too often called upon only in an emergency or in a belated attempt to mask inefficiency; too often confused with marketing or advertising.

This book aims to put this right by explaining what PR is and what it can achieve; how it fits into the overall marketing mix; how the media operates; what it regards as 'news' or 'feature' material; how you can use PR to establish better contacts with the media and feed journalists stories that will get printed or broadcast; how to deal with journalists; how to set up and operate a PR function or department; how to handle radio and television interviews; and so on.

The book is also indented as a valuable source of reference, giving lists of major national and regional newspapers and magazines and television and radio stations, designed to help you get the most out of your PR efforts.

Finally, I make no apologies for emphasising the media's major involvement in successful PR. Of course, PR covers a number of other tasks: in-company newspapers, the organisation of events, production of the annual report, even getting theatre tickets for the MD, but at the end of the day a PR department in the majority of cases is called upon to deliver targeted, positive, media coverage for its product.

'In 1865 it took 12 days for the news of Lincoln's assassination to reach London; during the Gulf War this year, we watched live coverage of the bombing of Baghdad. The Victorian postal service handled 76 million letters a year; now there are 13 billion. Between 1986 and 1990 the number of fax machines increased from 86,000 to 750,000. More information is estimated to have been produced in the last 15 years than in the whole of previous history.' (Recent edition of the *Independent on Sunday*)

Well, how about this. Donald Trump is reported to have paid nothing to a New York jeweller for the supposedly $140,000 engagement ring he gave to

Marla Maples. Both Trump and the jeweller were shrewd enough to know that the value of the gesture to each of them in terms of public exposure would far exceed the cost of generating similar media coverage through advertising, and indeed that advertising could never have achieved such exposure anyway. It is an intriguing example of marketing public relations in action as practised by a layman with an instinctive flair for self-promotion.

Crisis management. The story broke not so long ago that Perrier, the supposedly pure, unadulterated natural mineral water, was contaminated with benzene. The company faced potential ruin. There was a critical need for a rapid, effective PR programme to reassure the public and restore consumer confidence in the product.

Investor relations. Take the privatisation of British Gas. In support of a major advertising campaign PR played a key role in persuading journalists to highlight British Gas as a potentially rewarding and worthwhile investment.

Employee communications. British Telecom recently embarked on a major internal reorganisation. PR played and is playing a vital role in communicating the rationale to employees and customers alike.

And public affairs. Which politicians now dare to appear on television without some guidance, some training on how to present themselves and their images?

Let us stop for a moment and consider what we mean by publics. They can often be very small. Bob Dilenschneider in his book *Power and Influence* quotes an interesting example. In 1982 he was approached by the owners of the Three Mile Island nuclear plant in America. The film *Silkwood*, starring Meryl Streep, was about to be released and they feared the consequences. Dilenschneider was offered a million-dollar fee, but he asked for only five thousand dollars. His advice was that the owners of the plant neither needed to, nor could, effectively influence the general public. The number of people who could affect the owners' business and profitability and would see the film and be affected by it was only about thirty, and almost all of them were financial analysts. So the relevant public was very small.

If we look now at exclusively UK numbers, the PR consultancy market was estimated to have generated fee income of over £200 million in 1990. By the year 2000, our annual forecasts suggest that the market will have risen by at least 300 per cent. So the scope for increasing employment is very considerable, despite the temporary hiccup of the current recession.

As for in-house figures, a joint survey of in-house UK PR departments from 2000 of the country's largest companies found the leader of the field to be

WH Smith with a budget of £3 million. This trend towards a strengthening of in-house departmental budgets will, I think, continue.

There are currently, on the best estimate by the PRCA, just over 7,500 professionals working in PR in the UK. The grand total is 7,511 and it is broken down as follows: 4,877 in consultancy and 1,025 in-house, so more than four times as many people work in consultancy as in-house. Then there are 585 in the public sector and lastly another 1,024 working for other organisations, including charities, clubs and the like. As with the worldwide financial numbers, extrapolation abroad is more difficult because the PR industry is still so young that the figures are simply not available.

The 1991 total for UK in-house PR budgets of the top 50 spenders is over £39 million, which compares with 1990 total fee income of the top 50 consultancies of over £180 million.

If one compares the figures I have just given you – £180 million for the top 50 UK consultancies – with the worldwide figure for the consultancy market of £3 billion, you will see at once that it is now no longer the comparatively mature industries in countries like the UK and particularly the USA which will govern the development of the PR market over the next decade. It is the great growth potential in other undeveloped markets that provides the key to the future.

Think for a moment now about global communications and the enormous pressures for change that come with developing technology. I have referred to the international telephone or fax. Consider as well other forms of the international flow of information. News and information can no longer be confined to one geography. Indeed, in many cases, it is instantly available in many geographical locations simultaneously. You need look no further than the impact of CNN, the Cable News Network and now the BBC World Service television to see the point.

An outstanding example of the art of marketing PR occurred recently with the opening of the first McDonald's restaurant in Moscow. The planning for it began two and a half years earlier in 1988. It was certainly the biggest media event in McDonald's history. It was also arguably the broadest positive exposure any company has ever received, from the ensuing TV, radio and print coverage in North America to front pages and newscasts in Britain, Europe, Japan and the rest of the world. Canadian Broadcasting Corporation described it as the PR coup of the decade, and it was achieved through PR, not advertising.

To investigate the perceived relationship between PR and advertising, Shandwick, arguably one of the world's largest PR networks, commissioned research by MORI. The sample was 50 of the marketing directors or those with ultimate responsibility for marketing, in companies in *Campaign* magazine's top 100 advertisers and *Marketing* magazine's top 500 brands. The key results were these.

First, advertising is more likely than PR to be thought a marketing rather than a general management function; 96 per cent of those questioned thought advertising to be more of a marketing function.

Second, 60 per cent thought advertising and PR should be the responsibility of different people within client companies.

Third, 78 per cent thought that clients obtain better value for money with separate PR and advertising suppliers rather than both handled by the same supplier.

The trends that lie behind these figures are significant – an increasing recognition of the separate natures of PR and advertising, and increasing awareness of PR as an indispensable component in management rather than simply marketing.

Instead of being seen as mere editorial puffery, PR is coming of age as a vital tool of management – designed to help managers do their jobs more effectively and efficiently. It is about communications, here and now. Communications with staff, communications with trade unions, with the City, with markets and customers, and indeed between governments and those they govern.

All of which brings us to consider what are going to be the growth areas for PR in the 1990s.

1 *The nature of public relations*

Confusion about what public relations is and what it can, and cannot, achieve is still rife, so here is a selection of definitions, each emphasising slightly different aspects of the activity.

PR: SOME DEFINITIONS

- The projection of the personality of a company or organisation.

- The organised two-way communications between an organisation and the audiences critical to its success, the aim being to create understanding and support for its objectives, policies and actions.

- The management activity responsible for the creation of favourable attitudes among key audiences.

- An 'exercise in diplomacy': putting the facts and viewpoints of the client to whatever 'jury' is appropriate – government, the buying public, shareholders, a committee of inquiry, Members of Parliament or whatever.

- Something that embraces all the activities that build good relations with audiences, attempting to change negative or incorrect opinions and reinforce positive or correct ones. In other words, projecting a 'good feeling' for an organisation and turning the negative into the positive.

SCOPE

The 'official' definition of PR, from the Institute of Public Relations, is: 'the planned and sustained effort to establish and maintain goodwill and mutual understanding between an organisation and its publics'.

PR has many elements, publicity being one of the most important. This seeks to inform readers, listeners or viewers, and to be effective must have news value, something the media and PR professionals call a 'news angle'. A story must hang on a peg to be carried by the media; if it is of little or no interest to the audience it will not interest the reporter or editor, even if he or she is someone you have deliberately courted over the years.

Another element of PR is promotion, which also aims to inform, although existing mainly to project the benefits of a programme or product, and is more akin to advertising than publicity; this is why promotional articles are more difficult to place in the news media, since they usually lack a strong 'news angle'.

Although public relations is at last becoming appreciated as an important factor in the success of any organisation, some companies still engage in protracted discussions on whether they should 'have' PR or not. This is ridiculous, since all organisations are communicating with audiences that are important to them – in other words practising PR – whether they realise it or not.

The decision, therefore, is not whether to 'have' PR but whether these PR activities should be handled in a planned, organised manner or allowed to be haphazard, possibly inconsistent, and almost certainly ineffective and inefficient.

Increasingly, public relations is seen as an essential top management responsibility, not an optional extra or an add-on publicity gimmick, with companies and organisations now giving the development of a worthwhile PR policy as much thought, attention and professional skill as their financial or personnel policies.

Good PR certainly needs thought, planning and organisation. Indeed, while it should always be a welcoming host to bright ideas, it demands, if it is to be both effective and economical, as vigilant and exacting a programme of planning, preparation, timing and execution as any other job. Business, however efficient, must continuously study its PR needs and opportunities since it must not only be efficient but must be seen to be efficient.

However, PR is only ever as good as the product. The best PR will not compensate for weakness in business areas, and companies need to attract the right personnel and train, develop and motivate them.

The PR industry is making major efforts to train professional people to take on the most senior levels of responsibility, and the new generation of highly educated entrants to the profession expect to share corporate responsibility in the boardroom, alongside the established professionals such as engineers, accountants and solicitors.

Good PR people understandably want to prove their value by their creativity, their contribution to improved efficiency, greater commercial success, industrial expansion and better human relations.

PR officers or consultants can play a key role in building up goodwill, providing that their activities are within the framework of an agreed and understood corporate policy. The PR professional can help management to agree on the 'personality' that the company, corporation or organisation wishes to develop and project, and the practical PR actions that will achieve this.

Important groups of people, for example, tend to be overlooked when all is going smoothly, but when the going gets tough their goodwill may be essential. However, this is also the least appropriate time to appeal to them. Employees who receive proper communications when industrial harmony reigns may be much sympathetic when potential disputes arise.

In a nutshell, good public relations should embrace the professional strategy of planning in advance what opinion the public will hold concerning your product or organisation, because a carefully planned, comprehensive public relations campaign is the most effective and economical means of creating in the public mind a favourable impression or a desire for a product.

There is a tendency in Great Britain (although attitudes are changing), as opposed to the US where PR has been much more fully developed, to compare and confuse public relations with advertising. In fact, they are quite separate and distinct, and their impact on the general public is entirely different.

Advertising occupies space which the reader knows has been bought. No matter how attractively advertising material is presented, no matter how factual it is, it is bound to meet with some reservations: the manufacturer, whom not even the most generous and open-minded reader would consider impartial, has obviously got an interest at stake.

The art of public relations is to have the appearance of disinterestedness. It stands to reason that the facts regarding the merits of any company or product are more readily believed if they are put forward with apparent spontaneity by a person or body not directly concerned with increasing its sales.

It must be conceded that the image of the PR industry, until recently, was not good at all. People were very wary about PR companies and PR executives, and often quite justifiably. But, thankfully, the image of the PR man in the 1960s strutting down Fleet Street in pin-stripes and carnation to buy a bottle or two of Muscadet at El Vino's at lunchtime is now almost dead, not just because the 'action' has transferred from Fleet Street to Wapping and elsewhere, but because the PR profession has 'grown up' and journalists have grown up alongside it. The recession of the late 1980s and early 1990s has also put paid to the long lunch!

Today's journalists are much more willing to listen to the views of the PR executive than their predecessors, and most would admit that they would find their jobs much difficult were it not for the help and advice of professional PROs.

While the overall attitude towards PR is now much more favourable than before, several things irritate those in the industry about the way it is perceived, even by those with considerable experience of it. One such irritation is that PR is often seen as a luxury, to be indulged in only in times of prosperity, or, conversely, in times of emergency. In fact, it is especially important during a trade recession, ensuring that the public understands both the reasons for the policies being pursued and the difficulties that the enterprise is facing, and contributing directly to the removal of these difficulties.

THE KEY ELEMENTS

Put simply, then, public relations is all about communications, an over-used word but one whose importance should not be overlooked. And there are three key elements to the communications process, as follows.

What do you want to say?

The message is crucial. There is no point in using PR techniques for the sake of it. Your message may be to inform customers about a new product, or shareholders about planned activities; to tell employees about a factory closure or suppliers about a change in distribution patterns. Before putting pen to paper, or calling on the services of the PRO, establish what message, what 'angle' you want to try to put across. Bear in mind that it should be 'newsy' or controversial to stand a reasonable chance of making any impression or being taken up by the media.

Who are you trying to reach?

Clearly this must depend on the message you are trying to put across. But don't forget that there are many distinct and separate target groups that you should seek to influence. There are obvious ones such as your customers, but even this target group needs to be broken down into smaller targets: housewives on estates, to take one extreme, or customers for left-handed screwdrivers, to take another.

Then there are the not-so-obvious groups such as civil servants, MPs or local authorities, all of whom can make a major impact on your business.

Increasingly important is informing the financial community of what is happening. Good investor relations can help keep your share price up and be of crucial importance during takeover bids, either when you are on the defensive or the attack.

How can you get your message across?

This is where good PR comes into its own. PROs who are professional know which medium to aim for: trade or national press, or radio and television. They can also suggest when it will be more effective to use sponsorship, exhibitions, direct mail, or a combination of several, to do the job.

THE LESSON TO BE LEARNED

A spokesman for a major brewing compancy recently commented on his company's public awareness: 'Our brands are well known and that's what counts. We don't care if nobody knows the name of our company.'

Successive generations of financial journalists found out that the company meant just that; it was one of the most difficult companies to contact. Subsequently the company became very much in need of friends in the financial press when it found itself on the wrong end of a takeover bid from a major rival. In the end the price of saving itself from its rival's clutches was to be taken over by another company; one which had assiduously wooed, by all accounts, the financial press and institutions.

Effective PR will ensure that the public that is important to you is no longer ignorant of your good points, of your special strengths, your achievements and the difficulties that you are meeting and have overcome. The result of this increased knowledge will be greater understanding of your problems, greater appreciation of your achievements, greater interest in your business and quicker recognition of your products.

2 The role and function of a PRO

Once a company or organisation has decided to examine and tackle its public relations needs and objectives, there are a number of options available.

The three main ones are:

- The appointment of an outside consultancy.

- The nomination and training of an existing executive to handle the public relations responsibilities.

- The appointment of professional PR staff.

Sometimes the ideal solution may be a combination of more than one of these three methods.

One of the major factors in deciding which route to pursue will be the company's level of commitment to good PR. If it is operating in a competitive market, under public scrutiny, and possibly in a sensitive area, it will find PR absolutely fundamental to trading success, and will require skilled executives, whether staff or consultancy or a mixture of both.

Some organisations, such as companies with near-monopoly situations, statutory bodies, professional associations and some government authorities, may feel that they can relegate PR to a lower level of importance. Others have an equally narrow view of the role of public relations, giving their executives such limiting titles as press officer or, even more restricting, information officer. Clearly a press officer is responsible for only part of a broad PR function. Press relations, however effectively operated, are only a part of public relations.

Many organisations have to rely on voluntary or untrained assistance in PR because of the limits on their budgets. This is often the case with voluntary groups, churches, small charities, local arts societies and the like. But even with a very small or non-existent budget, PR techniques can still be employed to excellent effect, especially if there is a PR professional within the society or community who has an interest in the particular cause and can be persuaded to lend his or her expertise in a voluntary capacity. (See Chapter 10.)

Frequently the reason a PR budget is not available is simply that the company does not rate the importance of the PR function highly enough. If the management can argue that it does not need a significant PR resource, this may be an acceptable point for debate, but to contend that it cannot afford a proper resource is very questionable.

Effective PR ultimately costs no more than poor PR. The returns from an investment in public relations are usually so significant that a company has to be spending a very substantial amount of money before it reaches a point of diminishing returns.

THE CASE FOR A CONSULTANCY

The appointment of a professional public relations consultant can result in maximum impact. The size and diversity of the media is the overwhelming argument in favour of employing an outside consultant, for only a group specialising in PR can supply experts in the many different fields of publicity available today.

For a company to try to set up, within its own organisation, a department to cope successfully with all the outlets available to it can necessitate the employment of several senior executives, each expert in a particular field. The cost of this, together with secretarial assistance and office equipment, can be prohibitive for all but the largest firms.

Another handicap a company or organisation faces in trying to undertake its own public relations is that it is often too close to its own subject. The temptation to preach to people who are already on your side is difficult to resist.

An outside consultant, on the other hand, can take a detached view of your business and maintain a viewpoint of impartiality, and is in a much better position to present your case to the vital segments of the public you wish to reach.

ENGAGING A PR CONSULTANCY – THE TOP TEN TIPS

If you are planning to employ a consultancy, here are some guidelines:

- Don't let yourself be hoodwinked by wonderful, flashy, tap-dancing presentations.

- Don't be intimidated by great theorising on `market segmentations'.

- Question those bidding for your PR business closely on what direct media experience they have.

- Question who they know in the media.
- Question what success they have had in the PR field in the past.
- Ask to meet the account director(s) who will work with you.
- Talk to the media yourself for recommendations of consultancies you should see. Your trade media will be a good barometer in this area.
- See no more than three consultancies. If you can't make up your mind after seeing three, you never will.
- Suck it and see ... working with any consultancy in the early stages is always an experiment. Insist on an early review of the contract.
- Be wary of big international agencies except those with smaller regional offices. PR is a very personal business and you could get lost in a large organisation.

THE CASE FOR IN-HOUSE PR

Appointing an in-house PRO is becoming commonplace among large companies and organisations aware of the need to communicate effectively and creatively with the public and their own workforce. The advantages of doing so are obvious, not least the fact that the PRO is on hand most of the time to respond immediately to management's requests or briefings, and by being involved day-to-day in the company's operations can be totally familiar with all the developments taking place and all the areas lending themselves to promotion.

A skilled in-house PRO, therefore, can contribute a great deal to the way a company is perceived by the media and the public, especially if allowed to become actively involved at the policy-making stage when decisions are taken that affect the company's image and character.

Unfortunately, however, in a misguided attempt to contain costs, too many companies give the post of internal PRO to bright secretaries who, while almost certainly having the right personalities and right attitudes for the job, lack even the most basic of the necessary skills. As I hope this book demonstrates, the myths and mystiques surrounding public relations are largely imaginary but for it to be successful PR does require a great many skills and talents on the part of the practitioner, not least a thorough understanding of the media, something a promoted secretary won't have.

COMBINATION OF IN-HOUSE AND CONSULTANCY

An ever-increasing number of companies and organisations are tackling their PR requirements these days on two fronts: by establishing an in-house

PR department and, at the same time, engaging the services of a specialist outside consultancy.

The advantages of this dual approach to PR are obvious. Not only does it give the company or organisation peace of mind knowing that there is a PR practitioner just down the corridor who can be totally involved and immersed in the company, its plans and its developments, but in knowing, too, that it has the addded advantage of a pool of professional PR expertise to call upon to formulate and carry out skilled PR activities.

Engaging the services of a PR consultancy alone, without the back-up of an in-house PR department, can have its drawbacks, since account directors at most PR consultancies handle several clients at any one time, and there can be occasions when their priorities differ from those of the company paying the fee.

But even the `combination' approach to PR can come unstuck unless channels of communication and accountability are clearly established and monitored. The need for the correct internal set-up to feed the agency with good quality material to enable it to use its professionalism to best effect is vital. It is not appreciated how critical it is to establish the internal set-up correctly in order to get the most out of a PR consultancy relationship.

Of particular importance in this respect is the establishment of a central point of contact to deal with the consultancy and the myriad enquiries and queries that emerge. Unless the internal PRO is of sufficient standing and experience, this function should be allocated to a senior executive such as the marketing director.

Despite the possible pitfalls, however, a combination of in-house and consultancy PR does make good sense, and can be a very powerful tool if the set-up is right.

WHAT MAKES A SUCCESSFUL PRO?

Whether you opt for an in-house PRO, a consultancy, or a combination of the two, having the right person working on your behalf is obviously of prime importance. To help you in the selection process, here is a list of qualities, attributes and skills which, from experience, I believe are important in a good PRO:

- An ex-journalist or media person who has had some working knowledge of the media, and who knows and recognises its needs, as well as the tricks of the trade.

- Someone who has an uncomplicated approach.

- A person with a neat and tidy mind – a lot of PR is tying up loose ends, and administration.

- Someone who gets on well with people.

- Someone who doesn't mind being at the beck and call of the media for 24 hours a day. The communications industry doesn't work 9–5.

- Someone for whom *nothing* is too much trouble.

- Someone who can string several paragraphs together in their proper order to form an interesting story. Lack of this ability is the major complaint from the media.

- Someone who doesn't think he/she is God's gift to the media.

- Someone with patience and commonsense.

On the whole, the best PROs are, as I indicated, broadcasters or journalists who have been able to make that very difficult switch `over the fence'. They know how the system works on the other side, and that is a great help.

If, on the other hand, a new PR entrant's route has been via a university or college course, he or she should get into a radio or television station and a newspaper office – even for a day – to see how the system works at grass roots; see how a programme is put together; see how the columnist selects his/her topics.

There's a lot of new technology in PR, but technology won't help PR practitioners unless they understand the basics … what constitutes a story; how to interest the target media in it; and how to present the facts. Whatever path you take, the functions of the PR professional remain basically the same.

Beware the rip-off merchants

The bad image acquired by PR and the PR industry in the past in the UK is partly the fault of the practitioners themselves both in-house and in consultancies. That is why it has taken British industry a long time to realise the considerable benefits to be gained from positive and professional PR advice.

Of course, there are still rip-off merchants in our industry. There will always be people who will grab the retainer fee, blind you with science, but fail to deliver the promised media coverage.

But the industry is gradually sifting out the wheat from the chaff.

THE PRO'S JOB BRIEF

- To establish a PR information library; get together the important company news; and be ready and prepared when the media calls.

- To initiate media coverage of organisation or company activities, people, services and products through targeted media.

- To act as spokesperson for the organisation with no other member of staff being authorised to answer questions from the media, unless under clearly defined circumstances or as part of a planned media-briefing session; and to keep the number of people authorised to speak to the media as small as possible.

- To write and issue press releases to the relevant targeted media, whether trade, local, national or whatever, with approval of senior management being obtained before any release is issued.

- To keep in touch with media contacts.

- To plan an organisation's PR effort strategically.

- To be creatively tactical in the PR effort to, say, sell or move sluggish products.

3   *Costing PR*

Historically the public relations elements of the overall marketing budget has tended to be the 'poor relations' afterthought. This entrenched attitude has in recent years, however, been gradually changing as a more realistic understanding of the cost-effective nature of PR has emerged.

In considering the relative merits of developing an in-house PR facility as opposed to the use of outside consultancies, cost is frequently cited as a major influencing factor. This argument has been used as a justification in favour of both approaches over the years.

In truth, of course, this decision should be based on careful consideration as to how a company's image development and projection can be best served.

The smoke screen of cost is a common phenomenon and one which is frequently used in cases of major disappointment and sometimes serious problems when much-vaunted PR campaigns fail. Such failures can arise equally from over-generous as from parsimonious budgets. Lack of resources or over-lavish expenditure can, of course, be a factor in failure but the root cause will be elsewhere: in poor planning, execution or allocation of whatever budget *is* available.

Any sensible comment on the cost of PR must be prefaced by establishing certain parameters.

First, it must be assumed that PR is to be approached from a professional viewpoint. I have known many organisations – some very large – whose entire PR capability is staffed by junior personnel 'promoted' from other functions for a variety of nebulous reasons. This is not only a mockery of the whole concept of effective media and public relations, but serves to distort the perception of acceptable budget levels both at the outset and on a continuing basis as the results achieved fail to match up to expectations.

Second, if an in-house facility is to be established as opposed to use of a consultancy on the basis of cost, it is important to consider in the relative calculations all those ancillary costs so often ignored in such an exercise.

Remember that fees paid to a consultancy will cover not only salaries but all staff costs such as NI, pension, benefits, holiday pay, sickness and holiday cover. Also included are office accommodation, secretarial back-up, management and training.

Finally, if a consultancy is the preferred approach, it must be assumed that a professional selection appraisal has taken place and that the common pitfalls of performance-related contracts, executive time restricted agreements and offers of patently non-commercial fee levels have been avoided.

Public relations, as with most marketing disciplines, will have two distinct cost elements – fixed costs (salary and establishment costs of the in-house department or fees to the consultancy) and directly related operating expenses (telephones, travel, entertaining, photography, printing, etc.) The level of operating expenses is unlikely to vary significantly between a consultancy and an in-house department – they are those unavoidable necessities of operating an effective campaign.

In the author's experience there is a remarkably consistent relationship between the level of operating expenses and the fixed costs. For many years we have advised allowing an expense budget at a level of 30 per cent of fixed costs. As to salaries and fees, there are no rules of thumb as to what proportion of marketing budget should be allocated in this direction. So much depends on the size of the company, its objectives, the value placed on PR, the industry and the disciplines included under the general PR budget head.

It is true certainly that salary levels in the PR field have increased considerably over the past few years as the understanding of the profession has developed. This boom has resulted in a shortage of talented and experienced professionals who have been able to command even higher remuneration.

This position is further aggravated by a serious lack of proper training facilities for promising recruits. So much of the skills of PR can only develop effectively in an operating environment, working with a group of experienced personnel. Such conditions are unusual in anything but the really large commercial concerns, and most training and on-the-job experience therefore derives from consultancies.

Having invested much time and money in training promising newcomers, consultancies will fight hard to retain the best, adding further to the salary spiral.

There are some signs that the substantial influx of new talent over recent years has now provided the PR business with a satisfactory pool of labour and that there is now a more enlightened attitude to recruitment and training. This should result in more sensible salary conditions and avoid a repetition of the recent salary explosion.

What is now clear is that the cost of good PR personnel is equivalent to that of qualified accountants, solicitors, doctors and most other professionals.

In this environment, consultancies – faced with ever-increasing costs – have had to adapt rapidly in order to remain competitive. This is not unusual in today's climate but PR is and will remain a very labour-intensive industry. Personal contact – its most important tool – cannot be replaced by word processors and computers. None the less, a much more structured approach is now generally taken, with teams working on a range of accounts in order to make best use of scarce and valuable resources.

So, always remember that you get what you pay for in PR. There are no bargains. Many of the London consultancies with international links will tell you that their minimum fee currently is in the region of £35,000 plus expenses, while a medium-sized consultancy perhaps specialising in a particular industry will have a minimum retainer fee of about £20,000. You will probably meet a PR company that will be prepared to work for less than this. *But beware*: it will probably not have the expertise and will certainly restrict the amount of time spent on your work.

The best way, of course, is to decide on your PR budget, tell your consultancy and demand to know what you get in return for this. And then make sure that you have an internal system set up to keep track of your consultancy and see that you do get what you pay for.

4 How to deal with the media – Dunn's golden rules

Dealing with the media in all its forms is one of the most important and most difficult aspects of a PRO's role, and it is vital that it is handled professionally and competently.

Many people, including top executives, are wary of journalists, sometimes with good reason. Perhaps they have had bad experiences with reporters in the past, resulting in unfavourable or damaging publicity, or perhaps they simply instinctively distrust them. Whatever the reasons, there is no doubt that a great many people are reluctant to meet journalists, are cagey about giving interviews, and are generally suspicious of the breed, if not actually fearful.

MEDIA `MANNERS'

This is where a good PR officer can help, because he or she will be accustomed to press and radio/TV reporters; will be – or should be – on first-name terms with many of them, and will know what reporters are like, how they should be handled to achieve the best results; whether they should be invited for an elaborate lunch, or simply a glass of wine; whether a particular reporter accepts group media visits (many journalists don't, preferring to travel alone); and a hundred-and-one other things that can make the difference between a face-to-face interview or media visit being a success and resulting in favourable editorial coverage and otherwise.

But although effective dealing with the media is a skilled task, there are several rules wl.ich should be applied by anyone asked to give an interview to a journalist or simply in their day-to-day dealings:

- If a journalist telephones with an enquiry about your company/organisation or its facilities, ensure that the call is returned as soon as possible. The media works to tight deadlines, and failure to respond quickly can result in missed opportunities for media exposure.

- When a journalist is offered facilities, make sure that all the relevant departments/personnel are informed in advance of the visit as far down the line as possible.

- The author recommends *never* telling the media anything `off the record'. If you don't want them to know something, don't tell them. Many PROs disagree with this advice, so how you tackle this thorny problem is, therefore, a personal decision. Bear in mind, however, that it is the media's job to get a story, and although you may give your `confidential' information to only one journalist on the understanding that what you say won't be printed or broadcast, you never know to whom that journalist may subsequently talk, or what information may be passed on to some less scrupulous fellow journalist.

- When inviting media representatives for meetings, the PRO should do the necessary `homework' in advance so everyone is fully briefed on the nature of the publication or radio/television programme, and is aware of what angles the journalist is likely to pursue.

- Make sure you have a comprehensive library of good, clear, black-and-white and colour photographs of your `product ' and of yourself and senior department heads. Although colour photographs are more attractive and are being increasingly used in glossy magazines, the majority of newspapers and magazines still use black-and-white illustrations exclusively, for reasons of cost, time and technology.

- Don't keep chasing up journalists who have interviewed you or department heads to find out when the article will be published. It places them in an awkward position, and is usually a decision not in the writers' control but in that of their features editors, news editors or editors. By `checking up' afterwards you are only likely to cause, at worst, intimidation, or, at best, embarrassment.

- Don't over-indulge journalists with food or drink in the hope that you can `buy' good editorial. By all means be hospitable, but don't overdo it.

- Don't show journalists audio-visuals or videos unless they are professionally produced. Poorly made ones can destroy a carefully built reputation.

- Be very selective about the photos/releases you issue to the media. The fact that a `famous' personality has visited your establishment or bought or sampled your product is no guarantee that the media is likely to be interested in publicising the fact.

- Don't issue photos of people lined up in front of the camera holding drinks. Instead, try to be creative about photo make-up. (See Chapter 7.)

- Don't just mail out press releases to all and sundry and hope for the best. Consider the content of the releases and be realistic about those publications that are likely to use them. This implies close familiarity with the media and the type of stories and photographs they carry. The construction and use of press releases is considered below.

WHAT IS A STORY FOR THE MEDIA? – THE KEY ELEMENTS

So, what is a story for the media – or what happens when Joan Collins isn't news?

It used to be said that `Dog Bites Man isn't a story, but that Man Bites Dog is'. This, of course, is a gross over-simplification of what is a complex question, but does highlight one of the most important elements in determining what constitutes `news' and what doesn't namely interest value. A `news' story must be of interest; if it isn't it won't grab the attention of the reporter or news editor.

Another important element is immediacy. An event that happened a week ago is not `news' except possibly for weekly newspapers or periodicals. Study the national newspapers and you'll understand my point. Virtually all the news items, as opposed to the feature articles, will have an immediacy value: events or developments which happened the previous day or, better still, in the early hours of the morning. As far as national newspapers and radio/television stations are concerned, old news simply isn't news at all, and won't be published or broadcast.

Of course, what constitutes important `news' to one newspaper won't necessarily be of such importance to its competitors. *The Sun* or the *Daily Mirror*, for example is quite likely to give page 1 splash prominence to Joan Collins or Elizabeth Taylor and their latest boyfriends/husbands, whereas the same information will perhaps receive scant attention in the columns of *The Times* or *The Daily Telegraph*, if it is carried at all, that is.

Why? Because `news' has to be not only immediate but also of interest to the readers/listeners/viewers and the activities of Collins or Taylor may well be considered of paramount interest to *Sun* or *Daily Mirror* readers, but of little concern or relevance to those who read *The Times*.

So, what constitutes news largely depends on the media you are tackling. Is it local media, national media or your trade press? Is it the `quality' press or `popular' press? These are important considerations and you must be clear in your mind what audience you wish to interest, and whether your proposed `news' items, no matter how immediate and up-to-the-minute, will do the trick.

That said, the following story ideas would appeal to a greater or lesser extent to most sectors of the media:

- Major developments within your company or organisation.

- Revolutionary new products.

- Spectacular sales figures.

- Takeover bids or financial news.

- Research on your particular market or industry. You only have to look at the massive coverage that the building societies, for example, obtain when they issue house price surveys around the country, to realise this.

- Controversial statements by you on your industry. Always remember that journalists have newspapers/magazines to fill, and they have to fill them with interesting and lively `copy'. The more lively you can make your comments or observations within the bounds of the politics of your industry, the better.

- Expansion schemes such as new headquarters or factories. And, of course, these days – job creation!

WHAT IS NOT A STORY?

Once again, what is not a story depends on the journalist you are speaking to, and the publication or TV/radio station involved, but as a rule:

- Getting a celebrity to launch a new product at a vast fee does not always ensure media coverage except perhaps at a local level. The celebrity, especially a minor one, is not necessarily a story unless he/she has some particular and relevant connection or association with the product. You have to ensure that you build on the celebrity's appearance and the product, and `create' a news story.

Often, hiring a top celebrity can produce excellent coverage for the celebrity, but nothing at all for your company or product. Photographers may turn out in their droves to snap an `EastEnders' or `Coronation Street' star opening a new supermarket, but the chances are that, while the pictures of him or her may receive prominent coverage, nothing – or, at best, very little – is likely to appear in print about the supermarket, defeating the whole object of the exercise.

Treat celebrities for what they are: crowd pullers. They'll get the `punters' along, but you should build onto that appearance a good, positive media story – job creation or local environmental improvement, for example.

Remember that celebrities are ten-a-penny in the media world, and hiring one for that important opening or product launch could prove a costly mistake.

- Marginal increases in sales or performance targets are of little interest. Your figures have to show a spectacular increase, and if they don't it is perhaps best to talk about your industry's performance in general in a particular year, providing this can be shown to be spectacular or impressive, and weave into it details of your own figures and performance.

- A facility visit to a factory or new headquarters is seldom sufficient to provide good media coverage. Instead, you need to build on the visit by introducing new angles such as increased job creation or new equipment.

It is important to remember, too, that a company may sometimes be thrust suddenly into the spotlight of public interest when it does not expect to be, and on an issue that it has not anticipated. If its actions at that time are not presented skilfully – if, in fact, it is not already practising effective public relations – an unfavourable impression can be fixed so firmly in the general public's mind that it becomes difficult to shift.

Careful targeting of the media is required in the PR business. Blanket mailing of press releases is not effective PR.

At the same time it is not sufficient merely to have an interesting story to tell. That story must be `sold' to the media – whether it be a newspaper, an illustrated magazine, a film, a technical journal or a radio programme – through which it will make the maximum impact on the desired audience.

If you do decide on a media release, keep it short and simple with no adjectives and no waffle. But don't always resort to a release: most of them are thrown away, certainly by the cynical news editors of the national media. Instead, a telephone call or a short note setting out your story idea will very often produce much better results.

Also of prime importance is that PR practitioners should do their research before contacting a journalist or broadcaster to find out just what he/she writes about or what their programme is all about. *There is the story of the PRO who sent the radio reporter a photograph of a chair for inclusion in his programme!*

5 ▶ Setting up and operating the PR office

A comprehensive PR library from which to draw information for the media is a basic requirement for a PRO, and should contain the following:

- Short biographical details and photographs of the general manager, vice-president, chairperson, heads of department/executive staff.

- Detailed information describing your organisation/company/product in the form of one, or more, background releases.

- Specific press releases relating to individual newsworthy areas of your business.

- Photographs to support all releases.

- Lists of targeted media contacts including press, TV and radio.

PHOTOGRAPHIC LIBRARY

A PR library should contain black-and-white 8" × 6" photographs which can accompany and illustrate the content of your press releases, whether biographical or general.

The extent of the photographic library will depend on the business of your company or organisation. For example, a hotel photographic library should include black-and-white and colour slides of every aspect of the hotel, from the exterior to the bedroom and public areas. If your organisation manufactures consumer products, then your pictures should illustrate all of these. All photographic libraries should contain head-and-shoulder black-and-white pictures of key personnel within your organisation.

Update your library regularly. Keep track of colour photography requirements.

It is essential that the PRO should use a reliable photographer who can be on call at any time. If in doubt, your local newspaper photographers are often willing to undertake freelance work, and it may well be worth contacting the picture desk at your local paper. The whole area of photography is considered elsewhere in this book.

BIOGRAPHIES AND HOW TO WRITE THEM

Biographies and appointment releases should be short and concise. They should be written in the form of a press release, providing facts on the person's working experience, present position and relevant information on awards, hobbies, membership of any relevant professional bodies, marital status and age, although the latter is at the discretion of the person to whom the biography relates.

Extend the biographical details for your executives' local media – they may well be interested in what schools they attended. But take out all these facts when you send the biographical details to your trade, regional or perhaps national media.

Here are two examples of a biographical appointment announcement. Believe it or not, variations on the second version are still being issued to the media by PROs who should know better!

How to do it: specimen biography/appointment release

TOP HOTELIER JOINS ASIA'S
FASTEST-GROWING HOTEL GROUP

Asia's fastest-growing hotel chain, The Splendid Group, has appointed a top Hong Kong hotelier as manager of its new luxury hotel, the 500-room Hotel Splendid, Kuala Lumpur, Malaysia.

He is 30-year-old David Brown, currently manager of the award-winning Hotel Wonderful, Hong Kong.

The Hotel Splendid Group will have 22 five star hotels in operation throughout Asia within the next few months, making it one of the biggest in the region.

The Hotel Splendid, Kuala Lumpur, is located in the centre of the city's business and commercial district.

Facilities include an executive floor, complete with library, telex room and secretarial services. There is also a health centre with swimming pool and sauna.

David Brown, a graduate of the highly acclaimed Lausanne Hotel School, Switzerland, has held senior hotel posts throughout the world.

During his time as manager of the Hotel Wonderful, Hong Kong, the establishment won many awards for excellence.

Further information from:

[Contact name, address and telephone number]

[Date]

How *not* to do it: specimen biography/appointment release

MR DAVID HAROLD PETER BROWN HAS BEEN
APPOINTED TO THE POSITION OF MANAGER OF THE
LUXURIOUS NEW HOTEL SPLENDID IN KUALA LUMPUR

Mr John Robert Brian Smith, MCIB, HCIT, FNCL, Executive Director of the luxurious new 20-storey, 500-room Hotel Splendid, located in the heart of the fashionable commercial district of Kuala Lumpur, adjacent to the railway station, and Regional Vice-President Kuala Lumpur, Singapore, Bangkok and Hong Kong of the Hotel Splendid Group, which now comprises 12 different luxury, five-star hotels throughout Asia, today announced the appointment of Mr David Harold Peter Brown, formerly Manager of the luxurious 15-storey, 150-room Hotel Wonderful, Hong Kong, as new Manager of the Hotel Splendid, Kuala Lumpur.

Mr David Harold Peter Brown, who is 30 years of age and has been married five times, with 10 children, attended St John's Church of England Primary School in Wigan where he passed the Eleven Plus Examination before moving on to St George's Grammar School, Wigan, where he gained 5 'O' levels, and then attended the Wigan Catering College before going to Lausanne to attend the famous hotel school where he graduated with distinction.

After attending the Lausanne Hotel School Mr David Harold Peter Brown became a kitchen assistant at the Hotel Fleshpot, Soho, London, where after five years he rose to the ranks of sous-chef, before being named sous-chef with the Army Catering Corps, noted for its internationally famous cuisine.

After serving in various exciting Army locations, Mr David Harold Peter Brown joined the Hotel Wonderful Group, where he held a variety of positions, culminating in his position as Manager of the 150-room Hotel Wonderful, Hong Kong, to which he was appointed on 3rd March and which has since won some awards from newspapers saying that it is excellent.

31

The Hotel Splendid Group is one of Asia's fastest-growing hotel groups and it plans to open 10 new hotels in the course of the next few months. The Hotel Splendid, Kuala Lumpur, has a hairdressing salon, newspaper kiosk, air-conditioning, an executive floor complete with books, a room for telexes, and where secretaries will lend help, hairdriers in every room, sauna and swimming pool, coffee shop and shoe-shine boys.

Mr John Robert Brian Smith, MCIB, GCIT, FCNL, said today of Mr David Harold Peter Brown: 'I'm delighted to appoint Mr David Harold Peter Brown to the position of Manager of the Hotel Splendid, Kuala Lumpur. The Hotel Splendid, Kuala Lumpur, is trying to build a reputation for its cuisine, and I am sure that Mr David Harold Peter Brown, with his experience in the Army Catering Corps, will have a contribution to make in this respect.'

For further information:

[Contact name, address and telephone number]

[Date]

BACKGROUND RELEASES – THE MIDDLE GROUND

A background release is one alternative to the news release. Basically an information sheet filled with facts, it takes a middle ground between the discipline of a news release and a rambling phone call to a reporter or news editor, and is also used to supplement the basic information contained in a short press release.

Below is a brief summary of the type of information that could be included in a background release:

History of the company: The story of your achievements, of the people who have contributed to your development, the growth of your equipment and facilities, a sketch of your financial development and, if relevant, your company's present relationship with the community.

The product: The need it fulfils, how and why it was developed, how it compares with other products, how it is used, and the quality control methods in force.

Manufacturing: The story of the raw materials used and their origins, of the processes and techniques employed, plant facilities and equipment, and the economy and efficiency of the operation.

Marketing and distribution: Marketing methods employed, the extent of the product's distribution, transportation and delivery, unusual outlets, etc.

Research: A description of your laboratory and field facilities, the people engaged in research, your achievements, current developments and future projects, always stressing that research continuously makes products better and cheaper. Attention should be drawn to the work you do in co-operation with technical colleges and universities, government and other industries. The economic and political aspects of the research programme could also be mentioned.

Management: Personality stories about your top management could be prepared with special emphasis on their leadership in one particular field – production, employee relations, research – and on the part they play in local community life.

Welfare: The provisions that you make for employee welfare: canteens, pensions, training, safety, health schemes, further education, etc.

The product in use: A description of the type of people who use your product, equipment or process, where it is used, what it accomplishes and why it is used (such as cost, convenience, superiority, availability, prestige), the volume of use and its growth in popularity.

Preparing a background release can be more difficult than writing a news release because you must try to think of ever possible fact, and anticipate every question a reporter may pose. In addition, you should note unusual incidents involved with your event or the subject matter under consideration. Reporters and editors thrive on anecdotes, which can often bring life to an otherwise 'flat' article. Indeed, many feature articles begin with an interesting, unusual or amusing anecdote.

Preparing effective background releases

A loose outline format for backgrounders should begin with the essential information, with supplementary facts and figures added further down the page. If you discover interesting anecdotes, summarise them so the reporter can ask for details. You can also include short, tight 'quotes' that add colour to the story.

Try to keep background releases no longer than two or three pages, though you can attach additional data such as prior news releases, statistics, histories, biographies, diagrams, charts and graphs in an appendix if considered relevant. At all times keep the purpose of the background release in mind: to provide the reporter with *the starting point* for a feature story, or to complement a news release.

A well-prepared background release has the following advantages:

- It provides some control over the content and direction of the story. When a reporter writes a feature, the background release's outline may become the outline for the published piece. This is especially true when a reporter faces a tight deadline.

- It can help reduce the chance of errors being printed. This is because you have typed the facts such as names, titles, places and dates, and the reporters concerned can take all this reference material to their desks.

- It gives reporters more time to ask substantive questions and follow up on interesting angles, rather than waste valuable time gleaning basic information.

In short, do part of the reporters' job so that they can do a better job with the feature or news story. Your organisation should get a larger, more interesting article in return, and the media will thank you for your foresight. And that could lead to other stories in the future.

PRESS RELEASES AND HOW TO WRITE THEM

Press or news releases are the greatest bone of contention between PROs and the media because, quite simply, a great many PROs cannot write short, sharp releases. Most of them are far too long and waffle far too much. When you consider that the average trade paper receives in the region of 200 press releases a week (that number plus for the national press each day!) then you realise how competitive it is to get your release noted.

Having said that, releases stand a very good chance of being carried in the trade and local media, including radio, if they are pertinent and well written. Remember, too, that journalists understandably prefer receiving letters addressed to them personally as opposed to the anonymous 'The News Editor', so target your release to a *named* media contact where possible.

Reporters also prefer receiving news releases as opposed to backgrounders for the simple reason that they have insufficient time to write up your story from a string of facts. *In effect, the person writing the press release is doing the writing for the reporter.*

Ideally the article should arrive on the reporter's desk in a style and format the publication can send directly for typesetting. Few releases arrive that way, however, so what characterises those that eventually find their way into print or onto the air, and those that are swept into waste-paper baskets?

The chief reasons for releases not being used are: un-newsworthiness; lack of clarity; lack of detailed facts; and received too late. Thus, a release carrying all the necessary information is more likely to be used and, when used, more likely to be published in a more prominent position than one that doesn't. Reporters are human – despite what some critics would have us believe – and it is understandable that, if faced with a mass of news releases, they are more likely to opt for those containing all the particulars. If they have to phone up to extract even the most basic details, they're more likely to push the release to one side and forget about it.

So, every minute that a public relations person can save a reporter is appreciated and will create better media relations for your organisation.

That doesn't mean, of course, that most newspapers will use press releases verbatim. On the contrary, releases submitted by PROs are frequently 'followed up' by reporters not only to check the facts but often to dig deeper for a new angle to or elaborate on an existing angle that particularly interests them. This is especially true of the national media.

Press release style checklist

Newspaper and magazine writing is unlike anything you ever wrote at school or university, unless you studied journalism – and to confuse things even further, every newspaper and magazine has its own style. Thus, writing articles requires training and craftsmanship.

Many news releases are re-written by reporters, so the most important thing is to provide all the facts, clearly and concisely, typewritten, so the reporter can prepare the material for publication.

If, for example, you are dealing with one or two trade papers continually, ask the reporters with whom you will be liaising how they want material presented.

That said, there are several basic principles of copy preparation that most newspapers prefer:

- Type all releases double-spaced or $1\frac{1}{2}$-line spaced on printed News Release paper if available or on company paper containing the heading 'News Release'. Type on one side of the page only, and leave wide margins on either side. Double-spacing and the margins provide room for sub-editors' alterations and instructions, and typing on only one side prevents half of your story from being lost.

- Start the first page with the heading about one-third of the way down. This leaves room for an alternative headline and the sub-editor's typesetting instructions.

- At the foot of the sheet include the date in full, the name of the PRO as contact for further information, and the address and telephone number of your organisation.

- Limit your release to one or two pages.

- Include in the release the name and telephone number (including a home telephone number) of a person to contact for additional information.

- Remember the newspaper's deadlines: a 'news' release in the true sense is of no use if it arrives too late.

- Make the release newsworthy.

- Use simple sentences – and simple words.

- Tell the important part of the story first.

- Be specific: never use adjectives such as 'fabulous'. Likewise, personal opinions or insinuations should never be part of a press release unless contained within quotes. Give precise measurements or weights rather than simply 'large' or 'heavy'.

- Make sure names are spelt correctly; never use initials unless they are in the middle of the name; and include titles after names.

- Attribute information to a specific person. It gives more credibility to a story and also adds to its reliability. Avoid, if at all possible, 'A spokesperson said … '

- All statements and stories regarding the organisation should be approved by an appropriate authority.

- Use brief headings typed in capitals. Spell out numbers up to ten and use numerals for numbers over ten.

How to use a press release

A press release may be used in different ways:

- As a general news story for local newspapers and/or radio and/or television.

- As the basis for a feature story, perhaps in combination with a 'backgrounder' release. The news release, once received, may be handed to the features editor who will be expected to investigate the story further and develop a longer article to appear at a later date.

- As the basis for press conferences. These are held only to discuss controversial matters or to make special announcements, and consist of single meetings of the media with your organisation's spokesperson(s). Don't organise them unless they are absolutely necessary; press conferences are the ulcer-inducing part of a PRO's life.

- As the basis for a media event. Non-controversial yet newsworthy happenings can become the subject of a media event; for example a special function organised solely to obtain publicity, such as company celebrations or milestones or anniversaries. Unless *you* bring these events to the media's attention they will most likely go unnoticed.

- As the basis for a face-to-face interview. A personal interview between a journalist/broadcaster, the PRO and someone from your company will probably have been set up by you. Alternatively, as a result of your release the editor may have decided that a journalist should conduct a personal interview to discuss the release in more detail.

Developing a rapport with members of the media is the first step in establishing an effective public relations programme. The time spent gaining mutual trust and respect is your investment in future favourable publicity. If you know your media, you will know who is most likely to be interested in the story.

The good and the bad

Here are examples of how to write a press release – and how not to. The first example is how *not* to do it, while the second shows how the professional tackle the same topic.

How *not* to do it: specimen press release

CATCH! MAGAZINE COMMISSIONS MARKET RESEARCH
SURVEY INTO FISHING AND SCHOOLCHILDREN

CATCH! magazine, the exciting and informative partwork series published by Marshall Cavendish for the fishing enthusiast which was launched recently but already attracts a substantial readership, has commissioned marketing researchers Jonathon Bostock to undertake an independent survey into fishing and schoolchildren.

The survey came up with a number of truly interesting and fascinating findings, including the fact that both parents and teachers questioned by the Jonathon Bostock Marketing Research representatives were in agreement that if fishing were introduced into the school curriculum, children would be less likely to become aggressive or indifferent to their environment, while at the same time about 75% of the children interviewed, between the ages of 10 and 16, confirmed to the researchers that they would like to take part in fishing if the activity were introduced as a school subject, whether this took place during school hours or out of school hours.

The survey for CATCH! magazine also came up with the finding that almost half of the children interviewed did fish regularly (reflecting the fact that fishing is one of the fastest growing activities among young people) and while 80% of those were boys (which would seem to confirm the old stereotype), 55% of the children who said they would like to give fishing a try were girls, reasons given for not already fishing being due to a lack of opportunity rather than a lack of interest.

For all the children who did not already fish, the lack of equipment, fishing companion or opportunity were given as reasons – all problems, surely, which could be solved by organised activity at school?

None of the schools questioned already included fishing on the curriculum, although all were in areas where fishing waters are available, but approximately 80% of schools were in favour of the idea if funds were made available, and all teachers believed that parents would be in favour of fishing being taught, the children, too, confirming that 95% of their parents approved of the idea, with 49% telling the marketing researchers that their mothers and their fathers would much rather them fish than take part in any other sport.

Of the teachers interviewed by the researchers for the CATCH! magazine survey, 75% felt that fishing would improve their pupils' knowledge of the environment, bring them closer to nature and prove to be a calming influence, one teacher telling them, 'It is to be encouraged, it is a quiet, non-aggressive activity, not a "yobbo" pursuit.'

Finally, the survey findings indicated that the schools would be looking to local authorities to support the cost of fishing lessons.

Further information:

[Name of PR contact]

[Date]

How to do it: specimen press release

CATCH! NETS RESULTS OF FISHING SURVEY – COULD FISHING SOON BE ON THE SCHOOL CURRICULUM?

'Gone fishing' could well become a legitimate excuse for schoolchildren according to the results of a survey undertaken by CATCH! magazine.

The CATCH! survey reveals that both parents and teachers are in agreement that if fishing were introduced into the school curriculum, children would be less likely to become aggressive or indifferent to their environment.

And it is evident that the children agree. If fishing were introduced as a school subject, 75% of the children interviewed – aged between 10 and 16 – confirmed that they would like to take part, whether or not this took place during school hours.

Almost half of the children interviewed did fish regularly, reflecting the fact that fishing is one of the fastest growing activities among young people.

While 80% of these were boys – which would seem to confirm the old stereotype – 55% of the children who said they would like to give fishing a try were girls. Their reasons for not already participating were due to a lack of opportunity rather than a lack of interest.

The research was undertaken independently by Jonathon Bostock Marketing Research on behalf of CATCH! magazine, a new partwork series for the fishing enthusiast from Marshall Cavendish.

Further information:

[Name of PR contact]

[Date]

The effectiveness of the properly constructed press release is illustrated by some of the coverage obtained by it for the *Catch!* survey.

PART OF MAJOR COVERAGE OBTAINED FROM CATCH! *SURVEY PRESS RELEASE:*

National TV:

BBC TV – 'John Craven's Newsround'

National press:

The Star
The Mirror
The Daily Express

Radio:

'The Way It Is' – Capital Radio (3 minutes)

Regional press:

Evening Gazette, Middlesbrough (C: 70,000)
Sunderland Echo (C: 64,587)
Belfast News Letter (C: 97,000)
Express & Star, Wolverhampton (C: 227,932)
South Wales Argus (C: 450,000)
Oxford Mail (two items) (C: 42,471)
Huddersfield Daily Examiner (C: 41,000)
Ipswich Evening Star (C: 30,880)
Dudley Evening Mail —
Coventry Evening Telegraph (two items) (C: 81,000)
Birmingham Express and Star (C: 244,312)
Sandwell Evening Mail (C: 25,000)
Evening Echo, Southend (C: 59,513)
Scunthorpe Evening Telegraph (C: 22,703)

6 ▶ *Preparing feature articles*

Features are a more personalised form of journalism, allowing reporters more creativity than the news side of the media will permit, and thus holding more opportunities for the PRO. Here are some basic principles about placing feature stories:

- Let the newspaper or broadcasting station write the story whenever possible. Even if you have a writer on your staff, the media prefer their own reporters' writing. When journalists put time into a story it is a personal time investment, as well as that of their newspaper's so that resultant articles are much more likely to be used.

- A reporter will probably write a longer story, and is likely to think of angles and questions you might omit. More space, of course, usually means a bigger headline and more attention for your company or organisation and its products/services. One possible drawback is that you may lose control of your story. A lengthy news release or feature article presents all the facts in the order you would like them to appear in print, and it may run in a form similar to that which you submitted; this is not so, however, of a reporter-written story. The reporter starts from scratch and all kinds of things may appear in his/her finished article, some of which may even be embarrassing to your organisation or business.

Despite the possible drawbacks, however, this approach is usually worth it. Getting a reporter to consider a story on your company is half the battle; the rest is up to you to see that all the information and comments presented are positive.

Gaining the interest of a particular journalist in writing a feature article about your company or an aspect of its operation is not always possible, so syndicated or one-off feature articles conceived by you 'in house' and submitted to publications or broadcasting stations considered receptive and appropriate can prove an excellent alternative.

If you have an experienced journalist in-house who can undertake this assignment, so much the better. If not, you would be well advised to buy in the services of a journalist with some knowledge and experience of the subject matter involved, and here your trade media is a good source. PR professionals cannot be expected to excel at feature writing – a very specialised form of journalism – so it's always best to have these articles written by people who really know what they are about in terms of journalism and specific knowledge and background on your industry.

In addition to the journalist meeting your chief executive or senior officers to prepare a feature for the newspaper, you may decide to write your own feature, or have your PRO prepare it, for syndication to selected local or regional media.

FEATURE ARTICLES: CASE HISTORY

Here is a feature article entitled 'Looking for a Job? Don't Snub Hotels and Restaurants', prepared by a PR company for a trade association in the hotels and restaurants sector to highlight the job and career opportunities within the hotel and catering industries. It was written by a journalist engaged by the PR consultancy for the purpose, and was based on a lengthy meeting he had with the association's chief executive.

The article was used extensively by the media, either whole or as the basis for a follow-up by the various newspapers.

Reproduced here is the letter which accompanied the article and the feature itself, and the media coverage that resulted is also listed.

Specimen letter

Dear Editor,

I have pleasure in enclosing a feature entitled 'Looking for a Job? Don't Snub Hotels and Restaurants.'

You are welcome to use all or part of this feature free of charge.

The theme is particularly topical at this moment as the first Training Board careers seminar of the catering and hotel industry took place in London on October 19. Regional events are being held in Glasgow, Manchester and Birmingham over the next two months.

Also, the first major survey into wages and salaries throughout the hotel and catering industry is due to be published at the end of this month.

I do hope you find it makes interesting reading.

Yours faithfully,

[Name of PR consultant]

Specimen feature article

LOOKING FOR A JOB?

DON'T SNUB HOTELS AND RESTAURANTS, URGES THE
BRITISH HOTELS, RESTAURANTS AND CATERERS
ASSOCIATION

Local hotels and restaurants are crying out for staff – and hundreds of
well-paid, full-time jobs are going begging, according to the British
Hotels, Restaurants and Caterers Association.

Robin Lees, the Association's Chief Executive, claims scores of local
youngsters are missing out on job opportunities, largely because of
poor careers advice in schools.

'The hotel and catering industry, such a vital part of the nation's
tourism industry, now employs ten per cent of the 21 million people
who make up the British workforce,' he says.

'But the industry is battling against the entrenched attitudes and
inbuilt prejudices of careers officers, teachers and sometimes even parents, who still equate service with servility.

'Hundreds of opportunities exist for the skilled, semi-skilled and
unskilled, for school leavers and college graduates. Yet very many of
these vacancies remain unfilled because youngsters are being denied,
or are failing to capitalise on, the opportunity to get their feet on that
crucial first rung of the jobs ladder.'

Mr Lees says that one positive trend is that the campaign his
Association has mounted to change the image of the hotel and catering
industry and attract more young people – a campaign that includes the
staging of local seminars on career prospects in the industry – is working.

'The idea is to get the message over very strongly to 14-year-olds in
particular that the hotel and catering industry offers tremendous scope.
We are doing this by opening up the industry to them and showing
them what's available, and taking that through until they are 18 and
making their decisions.'

Mr Lees claims that, nationwide, the hotel and catering industry needs to fill 120,000 vacancies a year, with about 5,000 well-paid jobs going begging in London alone.

'We have seen London hotels sending people across to France to recruit staff, not for their accents but because they could not find anyone to take jobs that pay £100 a week. And these are real jobs, not a cosmetic exercise to tidy up the dole register.'

He concedes that the industry still has to establish its credibility as the major employer in the UK and as the tourism sector with the greatest growth potential.

'In 1986 nearly £2 billion was spent on capital investment in major tourism and leisure products in the UK. Of that, an estimated £338 million was invested in new hotels, and over £240 million was spent on hotel expansion and refurbishment – an investment momentum that is the best possible news for jobs.

'By the end of the decade the industry will have created 130,000 new jobs. Our aim is for staff of the right calibre to be drawn into these new jobs.'

Mr Lees says that of the 360,000 school leavers starting a YTS scheme this year only 11,000 entered hotel and catering – although the industry could provide 20,000 places annually.

He says there are many routes into the trade, depending on a person's ambition, whether it is to manage a restaurant or own an hotel.

Entry qualifications for the catering industry vary according to which branch is chosen, but three or four O-levels are a good start.

'The most important qualification, however, is personality,' says Mr Lees. 'Cheerfulness in the face of what can be long and unsociable hours, and the ability to get on with people, are extremely important.

'High-flying degree holders and YTS trainees alike can end up as managers within a few years if they show they have natural aptitude, and the possibilities for promotion and advancement are limitless.'

Mr Lees admits that the salaries of between £50,000 and £60,000 per year earned by top chefs in some of the country's most famous restaurants and hotels are very much the exception rather than the rule, but says salaries within the industry are by no means as poor as critics sometimes claim.

'Underneath the "cream" jobs is a pyramid with a career pattern that individuals can work out for themselves. There is an enormous range of jobs, skill levels and abilities, from those with no skills at all but who are keen and willing to work and advance themselves up the ladder, to well-paid jobs for trained and skilled people such as computer programmers and analysts who can contribute to, and gain from, this industry perhaps more than any other.'

He says that tourism is now one of Britain's major industries, with tourists to England, Scotland and Wales spending £13 billion last year; and it accounts for about five per cent of the UK's gross national product, employing, directly or indirectly, 1.4 million people, about one in every 15 of the labour force.

'Some people argue that "service" industries such as hotels and catering are being pushed to the fore at the expense of manufacturing industries. This is nonsense.

'Admittedly, the balance between them may change – indeed, is changing – but there is no question that one is going to supersede the other because there must be two pillars.

'What has been happening is not exactly a second Industrial Revolution but a movement which has created a service sector where jobs are likely to be more "real" and more long-standing than those in manufacturing.'

Mr Lees says the BHRCA has been working closely with bodies such as the Hotel and Catering Training Board in the provision of better training programmes for new entrants to the industry, including the staging of a series of seminars held in key centres throughout the country.

It is also stepping up its efforts to increase knowledge within schools and colleges of the career opportunities available in the industry.

'Not so long ago the hotel and catering sector was regarded as a candyfloss industry. Those days are over, thankfully, and the vital importance of the industry is now recognised by the government and the country at large.

'It only remains to convince school-leavers and young people that the industry is a worthwhile one to enter, and that it offers them excellent career prospects and good salaries if they are prepared to train and work.'

Further press information from:

[Name of PR contact and telephone number]

[Date]

HOTELS AND RESTAURANTS ARTICLE: MEDIA RESPONSE

National media

The Daily Mail (C: 1,700,000)
Today (C: 524,000)
The Guardian (C: 413,000)
The Times (C: 385,000)
The Daily Telegraph (C: 1,040,000)
The Daily Express (C: 1,540,000)
The Daily Mail (C: 1,700,000)
'The Jimmy Young Programme' (audience 2 million daily)

Regional media

The Evening Sentinel, Stoke-on-Trent (C: 99,000)
Bath & West Evening Chronicle (C: 25,000)
Evening Herald, Plymouth (C: 59,000)
Eastern Daily Press (C: 84,000)
Eastern Evening News (C: 45,000)
Reading Evening Post (C: 26,000)
Evening Advertiser (C: 34,839)
Dorset Evening Echo (C: 24,000)
Evening Chronicle, Oldham (C: 40,000)
The Western Morning News (C: 58,000)
Evening Post, Kent (C: 29,500)
Express & Echo, Exeter (C: 31,000)
City of London Post (C: 150,000)
Glasgow Herald (C: 119,000)
East Anglian Daily Times (C: 51,000)
Evening Gazette, Middlesbrough (C: 69,000)
The Star, Sheffield (C: 119,000)
The Doncaster Star (C: 71,000)
MS London (C: 125,000)

Trade media

Caterer & Hotelkeeper (C: 41,473)
Personnel in Management (C: 55,000)
Travel News (now Travel Weekly) (C: 27,000)
Catering South West (C: 18,500)

7 *Public relations photography*

One photograph, it is said, can be worth a thousand words. While the claim may sound something of an exaggeration, there is no denying the tremendous PR value of photographs. Photographs stimulate interest. Editors position photographs in their publications to give visual impact.

The first step is for you to have access to a few reliable local photographers who can be on call at any time. As local newspaper photographers are often willing to undertake freelance work, contact the picture desk at your local paper. Be careful about using one-person outfits; if you have to meet a deadline, it is of little value employing a photographer who will be unable to process the pictures until the following day because of his/her work schedule. The PRO of a large non-competitive company may let you have the name of his/her photographer, as will a local hotel with photographers for their conference clients. *Hollis PR Directory* has a section on PR photographers/photographic companies covering the country. Try out the photographers on in-house jobs before any major PR event.

When approaching a newspaper editor or reporter with a story idea, bring up some photo suggestions too; your visual idea may be rejected but you will get a feel for what type of pictures they prefer and it may even spark off another photo possibility which the newspaper *will* use. However, it is important to remember that while magazines and trade publications will use your PR photographs, most regional and national newspapers will want to take their own photographs and use their own photographers. All they will require from the PR department is convincing that a photo opportunity exists.

PR professionals, quite rightly, often spend hours of time working on 'photo opportunities'. Why? Because readers almost always notice photos, and that means the caption and accompanying article stand a better chance of being read; even if they merit only a cursory glance, you have gained more attention value than you would have done with a printed story alone. Do not, however, get carried away. Study the photographs used in your local media or in the nationals and you will see that very seldom do they blatantly 'plug' a product; that is left to the trade press. The photo idea must involve more than just an opportunity for you to plug your product. The skill is being able to incorporate the product either by the photo telling the whole story or the photo stimulating the recipient to read on.

If you are supplying the photographs remember to check whether the publication requires black-and-white, colour print or colour transparencies. For many years, colour reproduction in magazines required a colour transparency but nowadays new printing technology is moving towards the colour print.

Remember, press photographers are under no obligation to turn up to your photo-call – the picture/news desk may put them on a potentially better story at the last moment – so you must always have your own photographer present.

Your own photographer should be one of the first people you consult regarding a photo-call. Ask them how they would present the event photographically, discuss options and props. After all, they will know your product and the image you wish to project. They can advise you on the technical side of the photographic session; also your photographer can take the shots you want – the press may not.

If for any reason there is a safety aspect to the venue (hard-hat or no-smoking area, eye protection, etc), then be sure to hold a briefing session, both with your own colleagues and invited journalists/photographers to this effect prior to the taking of any photographs.

However, placing a photo in a newspaper or magazine is difficult for several reasons. First, most newspapers employing a photographic staff want to take their own pictures. The few non-staff photos used include agency wireshots (from AP, UPI, etc), 'mug shots' of executives in the business pages and – rarely – a publicity photo set up by a corporate PR department or PR consultancy. Enquire of those journalists turning up without their staff photographer if your own photographer can take an exclusive shot for their publication.

Then there is the lack of space. Photographic space is even more at a premium than space for words and there is considerable competition for it, so it is essential to use creative thinking if you hope to interest a newspaper in accepting and publishing one of your pictures, or sending their own staff photographer to take a picture.

Here are some tips to help you gain the most out of photo opportunities:

• The idea has to be good. Some stories have natural visual aspects, and the job of a good PR person is to bring these to the attention of a reporter or editor. As in all aspects of PR, don't waste the media's time.

- Planning is essential. You might have to create both a photo opportunity and convince people in your organisation that photos are worth their time and trouble. You may find yourself having to carry heavy props to a site convenient for a photographer. Sometimes, the photographer's schedule will not match your chairperson's schedule, so diplomacy and patience will be needed to achieve what you want.

- Dreaming up photo possibilities is more difficult than you imagine. Don't be too blinkered. Be sure to involve the person in charge of the project and if necessary 'brainstorm' ideas: have everyone submit suggestions while you note them. What you want are the unusual, or the incongruous, visual ideas. Prepare props in advance.

- It is also important to treat the photographer on an equal footing with a journalist: introduce them to the chairperson, guest of honour, etc. Often the photographs of the PR event are 'for the record', and no more. A good photographer will have special 'exclusive' requirements from your event; pay attention to them. A positive move is to meet with your local newspaper or trade photographer and have a general discussion on how to help get the best out of your PR event. Find out what sort of picture they will run with.

- Even if you have all the press turning out, you must still have the first photo planned. If it is good, the photographers will expand on the idea, otherwise they will quickly shoot it before moving on to their own ideas. A useful rule is to ensure your 'cast' are doing something: an action photograph is far better than a static photograph.

A few don'ts:

- Organisations and companies love photos of their officers shaking hands, probably with a chief guest. Newspapers, on the whole, do not. If you convince a hard-boiled newspaper photographer to attend your meeting/launch with only a handshake as a photo subject you will lose ground in your media relations.

- Likewise, the standard group photo is seldom interesting to anyone but those in the photo. Unless the photographer directs you to do something else, pose a small, selective group in an unusual setting. Remember the cardinal rule: newspapers want picture-orientated subjects, things that are unusual, good graphically, and tell a story by themselves. As a general rule, they do not like big groups of people, but much prefer two or three people in an animated and lively pose. This latter point applies to a number of trade publications.

Plan the photographic event carefully, considering interesting action shots you can suggest, and prepare your people to co-operate. The golden rule is to be punctual; photographers run on very tight schedules, and they usually allow no more than 15 minutes leeway for assignments. If your senior executives are late or you haven't got your act together, press photographers are unlikely to hang around until you are ready. They will move on the next appointment. Stress this important point to the central figures of your 'show', the chairperson for example. They will often say their time is more important than the media's. If they take this attitude it is fairly certain you will miss out on some valuable media coverage.

The time of day of your function is also an important factor – particularly in winter when 'photographic daylight' is at a premium: photographers often want to shoot outside. Allow time for processing prints if you wish to meet a deadline.

The photograph has been taken; now to present it properly.

An 8″ × 6″ photograph is usually the best size to use. Caption all copies of the photograph as follows:

- Type double-spaced, double-lined with wide margins on the lower half of a sheet of News Release paper, the date, location, names of people, their positions in the company and any other specific details, eg release/embargo date, contact name with 24-hour phone number, etc.

- Lightly glue the four corners of the photograph onto the paper above the caption.

- In case of a lengthy caption, stick the picture on the reverse of the sheet.

- Identify people by their full names and titles from left to right.

Finally, remember that photographers attend PR events every day of the week, every week of the year. The more you plan and prepare the shoot, including providing props, the more co-operation you will get from the photographers who will then be fighting on your side to get the photo used by their picture editors.

For the professional photographer's view on taking pictures that will get into the media, see Appendix II.

8 ▶ Press conferences, media events and interviews

In this chapter we look at meeting the media.

PRESS CONFERENCES

A press conference is an effective means of publicising to the media an important development within your company or organisation, but the pros and cons need to be considered carefully before you decide to go ahead with this particular PR approach. Journalists generally prefer 'exclusive' stories whenever possible, but if you have a major announcement to make, a press conference is an efficient way of doing so. Economics these days make press conferences an expensive business, especially if paying for rooms or hotels is involved, so only have a press conference if your news is vital or if you feel that, once a year, your senior executives should meet the media for a mutually beneficial exchange of ideas and thinking. If this is the case, then be honest with the media and say they are being invited for an 'update briefing'.

If you do decide to arrange a press conference, follow these guidelines:

- When to schedule? Check that the date does not coincide with another major press conference or local media event. Get in touch with the news editor of the local newspaper or radio/television station, or your contacts on the national or trade press; they should be able to advise of any conflict in times.

- Who to invite? Invite the news editors of all media in your area including any special interest magazines. They will allocate an available journalist. Also invite, personally, your own media contacts. Local dignitaries or officials and other community opinion leaders should also be invited if appropriate. But remember, it is media publicity you are seeking, so the media and its requirements should come first. The other danger in inviting local dignitaries or officials is that the media may uncover another and perhaps better story or angle which could overshadow what your people have to say.

Issue printed invitations – or personally addressed, and signed, letters of invitation – in plenty of time. If the conference is designed to produce a 'news story', make the letter as enticing as possible without going overboard.

Specimen letter of invitation

[Date]

[Address]

Dear

Happy Holidays launches 1994 programme

Tuesday, 16 February 1993

Happy Holidays, the UK's leading domestic tour operator, has expanded its 1994 summer programme by 30%.

I should be pleased if you can attend a press conference on **Tuesday, 16 February 1993** where John Smith, Managing Director, Happy Holidays, will be revealing full details of the new programme and discussing the strategy behind it.

The conference will start at 12.30 for 1.00 pm at the Holiday Inn Mayfair, Berkeley Square, London, W1. It will be followed by a buffet lunch and the opportunity to meet other key Happy Holidays executives including Joe Bloggs, Finance Director, and Tom Brown, Sales and Marketing Manager.

If you have any further queries, please do not hesitate to call me or my colleague, Louise White. Our direct line is 071-456 8345.

I do hope you will be able to join us on the 16th and look forward to seeing you.

Yours sincerely

[Name]

[Title]

- Two days before the event, telephone those who have not replied and compile a list of acceptances. Watch the timing of this call. It will irritate the media if you ring about the reply just when they are going to press. Research the best time to ring your media: in the morning or late afternoon?

- Prepare a typed outline of the form the conference is to take, and present it to the media on arrival. Don't make the kit too bulky; it is not necessary to include every item of publicitly material from your organisation, only that which is relevant.

- Ask attendees to sign or rather *print* their name in a visitor's book so that you have a record of who attended, and, equally important, who did not, so you can arrange for the information to be sent or delivered to the absentees by messenger as soon as possible but check whether they require it – you may be wasting your time and money.

- Prepare a press release which details the subject of the press conference, and include this in a press kit which should be distributed on arrival.

- Arrange speakers at a table on a dais with large cards in front of them clearly indicating their name and title.

- Ensure that the media briefing is short and to the point.

- If radio and television coverage is required, discuss the facilities needed in advance of the day. Make sure a visual identity of the organisation's name is placed in such a way that the cameras cannot help but pick it up and give you valuable free publicity, eg a company banner/sign behind the dais where the speakers are sitting. This is used most effectively these days by hotels when press conferences are televised.

- Embargoes. You may wish to give your story in advance to a contact who cannot attend your conference. An embargo means that the media should not print or broadcast your story until after the time you have stipulated, eg 1.00 pm if your conference is set for 12.30 for 1.00 pm. Very rarely has the media broken an embargo – until recently. Sadly, because of circulation wars and the breakdown of the 'unwritten rule' principle, many newspapers are now breaking embargo deadlines. So be careful – you really can't trust the media, at least in this area.

MEDIA EVENTS

This is an informal gathering of the media to cover an event staged by your company or organisation, such as a celebration or anniversary, where, for example, local newspaper photographers are invited to capture the event.

Invitations must be sent to news editors of local papers, radio and television stations, and it is also advisable to send an invitation to the picture editors of the local newspapers since it is they who control the staff photographers and decide which photographs will be used in the newspapers.

A news release should be given to all media, including the photographers, on their arrival. This should give details of the event, the organisers, and any other relevant information.

FACE-TO-FACE INTERVIEWS

Face-to-face interviews are among the best means available of obtaining good media coverage, and are generally much more effective than large-scale press gatherings. This is because, as indicated earlier, journalists, especially news editors, prefer 'exclusive' stories and angles wherever possible, and are much more likely to 'spike' or play down stories which they know other newspapers have also been given (unless, of course, the story is so sensational and important that they would be failing in their duty to their readers by not reporting it in full).

Many journalists will not ask their most important questions at a conference in front of their competitors for fear, quite rightly, of giving away their own particular 'angle' and will often seek out a face-to-face interview immediately after the formal press conference; so be prepared. Since most companies' stories are not earth-shattering, face-to-face interviews will generally produce better results, and if the right reporter from the 'right' newspaper or magazine – that is, the medium in which coverage of your company would be most advantageous – is invited, excellent results can be achieved.

It is also worth remembering that important local or trade media may merit a private briefing, embargoed, before that major press conference.

Once the particular newspaper/journalist has been identified for the face-to-face briefing, the following guidelines should be applied:

- The PRO should be familiar with the publication/radio/television programme the journalist works for and its type of readership/audience. If a radio or TV station wishes to conduct a live interview it is quite acceptable to ask the journalist involved the nature of the interview and what questions are likely to be asked. In this way the PRO can research the answers to be given by the interviewee.

- Make sure a positive message is included within the written news release, which should be given to the journalist before the interview is undertaken.

- Use notes on the subject under discussion; do not rely on memory. Give the journalist a full press kit before the interview so that all the facts are to hand.

PRESS LUNCHES

Hosting a media lunch can be an excellent way, apart from a press conference, of announcing news and giving updated information on your product, and especially effective if it is an informal occasion that gives both press and the company/organisation the chance to discuss points of mutual interest face-to-face.

However, it is important to remember that the last thing most journalists need is yet another free lunch – most are inundated with lunch invitations every day – so the letter of invitation must include details of the reason for holding the event, such as the story to be discussed, and indicate that the event will give the media the opportunity to question the client directly. The letter of invitation, in fact, is of paramount importance, since it can stimulate a news editor's or journalist's interest, or do the opposite. Great care and thought should be given to its composition, therefore, in order to create an aura of interest and importance to the planned event and thus provoke a firm acceptance.

In order to maintain a well-balanced client/media guest list, it is advisable not to exceed, say, ten press and three client representatives who are of management status.

Media lunches are best arranged in a private room of a restaurant or hotel. All media representatives should be given a press kit on arrival, giving details of what is to be announced. Lunch is normally preceded by cocktails/open bar, and is an ideal time for both client and media to meet.

Speeches are best delivered before lunch, allowing the actual time during lunch for continuing discussions, and for the media to leave early if they wish.

Ensure that the timing of the event is punctual; do not allow it to run on until late afternoon, since this will only irritate and inconvenience the journalists. A suggested timetable could be: 12.30 Drinks, 12.55 Speech, 1.00 Lunch, 2.30 Finish.

Whoever is making the speech should be briefed by the PRO beforehand on what 'angle' the journalists are most likely to be interested in, what things to avoid saying or to play down, what awkward questions might be asked, and the appropriate replies to them.

It is advisable to rehearse a 'question and answer' session with your executives in advances. Think of and plan the answers to all the negative questions.

MEDIA VISITS

Hosting a media group requires a great deal of personal time, involvement and patience on the part of the PR officer. But the benefits of this kind of PR activity are numerous, the most obvious being that you have a group of journalists as a captive audience, comparatively ready and willing to be given stories and news for as long as they are your guests. It is, therefore, vital that their visit is planned and co-ordinated with meticulous detail.

Whether the journalists are being invited to view your hotel, experience your country, see the manufacture of a new electronic product, or attend the opening of a new factory for two days or five, the organisation of their visit should be based on the same concept, and the same basic rules applied.

First, decide why it would be beneficial for you to invite a number of the media at one time. What story do you have to tell that is best experienced at first hand by the writer, rather than told in the form of a press release or feature article?

Decide which category of media you wish to reach and research the names of the relevant correspondents who might be interested in writing about your product. If they are regular media contacts of yours then your job is easier; if not, you should write to the editor of the publication suggesting that they may wish to nominate a representative to participate in the visit.

It is important that any media group is kept small – the ideal number is six, with ten as the maximum – in order that each can receive personal attention from you.

In the official letter of invitation outline the purpose of the visit and the itinerary, and indicate dates and the duration of their stay. If at this stage you can confirm their travel arrangements, give details; otherwise it is acceptable to supply these later.

The PRO should be prepared to be present with the group at all times, unless specified in the itinerary. It is also important to ensure that the schedule includes details of when the journalists will be expected to pay their own expenses. This usually occurs during free time when appointments are not scheduled.

Include in the itinerary details of all official appointments, breakfasts, lunches and dinners that will be hosted by your organisation or other officials. Give details of times when you require the presence of the journalists and indicate where and when particular codes of dress are required.

As an additional aid, it is always helpful to advise on the local temperatures, especially if journalists are visiting from overseas, so that they can adjust their wardrobe requirements.

Media visit checklist

Do:

- Keep the size of your group to a number that can be easily handled by you.

- Make sure the itinerary is an interesting combination of work and pleasure.

- Be prepared to be on duty 24 hours a day. Journalists like to think they have the right to call on your advice at any time, and invariably do!

Do not:

- Plan a media visit that lasts five days when the itinerary can be accomplished comfortably in three.

- Waste journalists' time. If they cannot think of anything to do during their free time, advise them of the interesting options.

- Do not overload the itinerary. Remember that the media are human!

9 *Effective PR use of radio and television*

Because of the increasing importance of television and radio in the battle for PR success, this chapter is devoted to giving the background to television and radio in the UK, describing their functions, roles, and the audiences for whom they cater – essential knowledge for anyone involved in PR.

INTRODUCTION

Without detailed knowledge of what is likely to interest a particular programme and what is not, a great deal of time and expense can be wasted sending inappropriate press releases and invitations. So no apologies for going into the subject in some depth.

Basically, radio and television in the UK is divided between the services offered by the British Broadcasting Corporation (BBC) and commercial stations controlled by the Radio Authority and Independent Television Commission.

In 1993 a number of new licences were granted by the government for commercial television operations. This brought in new staff, producers, formats and policies and meant considerable re-research and updating of contacts for PROs.

The BBC began in 1922 as the British Broadcasting Company, and received a Royal Charter as a Corporation in 1927.

Local radio began with an eight-station experiment in 1967 and was expanded to 32 stations by late 1984. The network is still growing.

The Radio Authority is the central body responsible for the provision of independent local radio services in the UK. It came into being on 1 January 1991 with the introduction of the Broadcasting Act 1990. The Independent Television Commission also came into existence on 1 January 1991. It is the public body responsible for licensing and regulating commercially funded television services provided in and from the UK.

THIS IS THE BBC

The BBC's principal objective is to provide broadcasting services for general reception at home and abroad. As an organisation, the Corporation is governed by a Royal Charter, which defines its objectives, powers and obligations, its constitution and the sources and uses of its revenues.

A Licence and Agreement granted by the Home Secretary alongside the Charter prescribes the terms and conditions of the Corporation's operations. Subject to the general law of the land, and the provisions of the Charter and Licence Agreement, the BBC has full editorial and managerial independence in its day-to-day programmes and other activities.

The BBC may not express a view of its own on any matter of public controversy or public policy as required under the terms of the Licence. However, as a former director general said 'We have to balance different points of view in our programmes, but not necessarily within each individual programme. Nothing is more stultifying than the current affairs programme in which all the opposing opinions cancel each other out. Sometimes one has to use that method, but in general it makes for greater liveliness and impact if the balance can be achieved over a period, perhaps within a series of related programmes.' That remains BBC policy today.

The BBC relies on two principal sources of income:

• A licence fee for colour television set owners and for black-and-white set owners covers the radio licence. Those who use radio but do not own a television do not have to pay a separate licence fee.

• Services for overseas listeners: the World Service is financed by a Grant in Aid from the Treasury; in other words it is paid for by the taxpayer.

The BBC is forbidden by its Licence to obtain revenue (for any consideration in kind) from the broadcasting of advertisements or from commercial sponsorship of programmes. In this context the BBC's policy is to avoid giving publicity to any individual person or product, firm or organised interest, except in so far as this is necessary in providing effective and informative programmes – something the PR practitioner should constantly bear in mind.

However, this is a *very* grey area. Increasingly, as budgets get tighter, there are enormous opportunities for PROs to obtain valuable visual and verbal credits for their products as producers seek indirect sponsorship of their programmes. This can come in the form of travel facilities, location suggestions or products to be used in a programme, eg cars etc.

BBC RADIO

The BBC provides five national services: Radio 1, Radio 2, Radio 3, Radio 4 and Radio 5; and four national regional services: Radio Scotland, Radio Wales, Radio Cymru (Welsh language) and Radio Ulster.

In England and the Channel Islands, local services are provided by 32 local radio stations, offering immense PR opportunities. There are national regional radio stations in Scotland, Wales and Northern Ireland with local or community stations which 'opt out' of these services to provide programmes of local interest.

BBC Radio 1

Aimed at youth, Radio 1 is mainly a pop and rock music station, attracting 16 million listeners throughout the UK.

The network also provides its young audience with practical help on specific problems which usually consist of intensive week-long campaigns or major documentaries covering a wide range of subjects from school and careers guidance to drug abuse. These take the form of on-air bulletins, backed up with 'freefone' advice lines and information packs.

Radio 1 listeners also have a regular news programme, 'Newsbeat', broadcast at 12.30 pm and 6.00 pm daily. Other features include 'The Radio 1 Roadshow' which tours seaside resorts, broadcasting live from different locations during the summer months.

PR opportunities out of the 'pop' music area on the network are limited unless they are of national interest, but the producers are always interested in talking to PROs about interesting destinations for the Roadshows.

BBC Radio 2

Radio 2 is on the air 24 hours a day, broadcasting popular light and specialist music, comedy and entertainment shows, as well as hourly news bulletins, traffic and weather information, to around 11 million listeners.

The all-star line-up of presenters has a distinctive and easy conversational style – ranging from the wit and whimsy of Terry Wogan at breakfast, the music shows of Sarah Kennedy, Ken Bruce and Ed Stewart, and Gloria Hunniford's celebrity interviews, to the probing approach of the Jimmy Young and Brian Hayes current affairs shows which talk to the people making the news.

A number of opportunities exist here for inclusion in various shows, especially the Jamesons' and John Dunn programmes both of which are

interested in ideas for locations for outside broadcasts. 'Hayes Over Britain' is Radio 2's Tuesday night phone-in show and the network's social action team prepare campaigns throughout the year on such subjects as redundancy, volunteering, crime prevention and health care.

BBC Radio 3

Radio 3 devotes nearly 85 per cent of its output to specialist music, primarily classical, although there are special programmes for jazz and traditional music followers. Like the other BBC radio networks, Radio 3 carries regular news bulletins, and in addition broadcasts plays, poetry, arts, news and features and shares live commentaries on international cricket matches with Radio 5.

The majority of the programmes are listened to for their high academic interest, and on the whole only music PROs need apply!

BBC Radio 4

The backbone of Radio 4 is news and daily current affairs. 'Today', 'The World at One', 'PM', 'The Six O'Clock News', 'The World Tonight' and 'The World This Weekend' feature among programmes made by over 20 different production departments and attract a significant proportion of Radio 4's nine million listeners a week. It is these programmes that are of significant interest and importance to PR practitioners, who should make a point of getting to know the producers and editors involved and the type of input they are constantly looking for.

All these programmes are open to PR 'news' ideas and the producers and editors regularly send representatives to press conferences as well as take in regional contributions. To get airtime on 'Today' is a coup for any PRO; after all, even Prime Ministers listen to this (though only before 8.00 am!).

When Parliament is sitting, Radio 4 broadcasts a record of its proceedings in programmes such as 'Today in Parliament' and 'In Committee'.

BBC Radio Drama is the single largest patron of new playwriting in the UK, broadcasting at least one play a day plus series and serials, both classical and contemporary. Radio 4 also covers medicine, science, sport, religion, business, holidays, finance, music and arts topics in its regular series.

Phone-ins offer direct lines to Presidents and Prime Ministers, or simply to an expert on a popular hobby.

Although Radio 4 does not attract the highest audiences, it reaches middle-class, middle-aged listeners: prime targets.

The network also offers a variety of current affairs, talks, documentary and science programmes, light entertainment, including a number of acclaimed comedy series, and some of the best drama and poetry around.

BBC Radio 5

Radio 5 is the sports network and also broadcasts schools, education, children's and youth programmes.

The network provides live coverage of most of the major sporting events including national and domestic football, the Olympics, the Rugby World Cup, Wimbledon, racing and cricket. Its programming is flexible to allow for coverage of events at short notice.

There is also a broad range of programmes, from magazine shows aimed at adults, to youth drama, comedy and readings for children.

There are plenty of PR opportunities in the pop and rock area: Johnnie Walker's 'AM Alternative' regularly features live acoustic performances, the 10.10 pm strand of youth magazine shows has live sessions and pop guests and 'Vibe!' is aimed at a teenage audience. 'Popcall' is a phone-in quiz with CDs, tickets etc useful for prizes ('Sportscall' ditto but for sports-related items).

The weekend morning shows are for younger listeners and go for the 'poppier' end of the market. These shows are also interested in relevant video/book/film material to suit the audience.

BBC Radio News

BBC Radio News reports 24 hours a day, 365 days a year, bringing listeners news reports and up-dates with over 100 broadcasts a day. Editors assess incoming news from the BBC's own staff and from world news agencies such as Reuters, as well as from PR professionals. Outside Britain, BBC Radio News has a network of foreign correspondents, based in the world's major capitals, sending to London reports of news as it happens.

The station also sends an hourly service of national and international news to the BBC's local radio stations and regional newsrooms in Wales, Scotland and Northern Ireland. In turn, these stations submit news from their own areas to the London newsroom, providing a continuous exchange of information. Industry, defence, arts and science are among the areas of interest covered by specialist correspondents.

BBC Local Radio

BBC Local Radio's 39 stations in England provide a speech-based, journalism-led service of news and information to local audiences, reflecting the issues and concerns of the communities they serve.

Around ten million listeners a week tune in to their local BBC stations, each of which broadcasts around 18 hours of local output a day.

The stations provide core information services such as traffic, travel, local weather, sport and leisure activities and act as a focal point for community debate and action on the issues that matter to the area. In emergencies or bad weather, they become a life-line for communities when they are frequently the only source of news.

BBC Local Radio provides something of interest for everyone, whatever one's age, interests or needs. Programmes for younger listeners, for example, broadcast job vacancies and give information on education courses. The stations provide the country's multi-racial and multi-lingual groups with a radio voice in the community, broadcasting around 200 hours a week in more than a dozen languages for ethnic minority communities in England.

In addition to local radio services in England, the BBC also provides a full range of radio programming for listeners in Scotland, Wales and Northern Ireland. BBC Radio Scotland is the country's only national radio network, broadcasting 9,000 hours each year. A separate radio service, Radio nan Gaidheal, broadcasts 1,500 hours a year to the 60,000 Gaelic speakers in Scotland. In Northern Ireland, BBC Radio Ulster broadcasts 90 hours each week and its local opt-out station, BBC Radio Foyle, broadcasts 1,200 hours a year to the Northwest of the Province. BBC Wales is the national radio service for Wales, broadcasting 100 hours a week in the English language. BBC Radio Cymru is its Welsh-language counterpart, also broadcasting 100 hours a week, and listeners in Northeast Wales receive a service of local news, weather and travel from BBC Radio Clwyd, the local opt-out service of Radio Wales.

There is a host of other radio stations opening up – London alone has 18 radio stations including the BBC. Specialist stations like Jazz FM and Classic FM – where most of the programmes are sponsored – are proving very popular. Classic FM has five million listeners a week.

THE SYNDICATED TAPE

Local media is a goldmine for PROs. With so many hours to fill and, in some cases, a shortage of staff because of budget restrictions, local radio is wide open to PR ideas for news, phone-ins, tips, hints on gardening or interior design; in fact, practically every subject under the sun.

It is here that syndicated tapes come into their own. These are produced by independent production companies in conjunction with PR departments. They last about three minutes and are mailed to radio stations in much the same way as press releases. The stations are given a typed intro to the tapes for the broadcaster to read out. The tapes can 'plug' but very subtly.

The take-up varies depending on the subject, but a 50 per cent usage is above average. They are generally *not* used at peak times, but often do get repeated.

There are agencies which provide a 'down the line' service to PROs and their clients. This service links selected radio stations of a central studio, perhaps in London, with interviewers live at the local stations. This service is preferable to the syndicated tape as you *know* that your client or chief executive is being interviewed live.

INDEPENDENT LOCAL RADIO

Independent Local Radio is governed by the Radio Authority which replaced the Independent Broadcasting Authority on 1 January 1991, following the introduction of the Broadcasting Act 1990.

Independent broadcasting is completely self-supporting; no income is received from licence fees or other public funds. The individual radio stations obtain their revenue from the sale of advertising time in their own areas, and pay the Radio Authority a licence fee to cover its cost in administering the system.

There are 90 independent radio stations and 143 services (some radio stations operate split AM/FM services), providing audiences with locally relevant programmes fashioned to suit their particular needs and interests. Concise news bulletins and short features, music and entertainment items make up the 'mixed daytime' programming style of ILR. This broadcasting is seen as a utility to be dipped in and out of, to fit in with the pattern of the listeners' daily lives.

Each station is able to keep a watching brief on what is happening in its locality and can report quickly on the news, events, traffic and weather conditions of the area it serves.

Local radio stations can 'buy in' international and national news bulletins from independent agencies such as Independent Radio News and Network News.

SUMMARY

The average amount of listening to radio per head per week is about 21 hours: 59 per cent of radio listeners choose BBC stations, while 31.9 per cent listen to local commercial radio and 5.5 per cent to national commercial radio. (BBC World Service, etc., makes up the remaining 3.6 per cent.)

Daily peak listening time is generally the early part of the morning. Of radio listeners interviewed, on average 46 per cent claimed to listen every week-day at some time between 6.00 am and 9.00 pm. A further 19 per cent said they listened most mornings, while 10 per cent listened occasionally at this time. The remaining 25 per cent said they never listened to the radio at breakfast time.

BE EFFECTIVE ON RADIO OR TELEVISION

In these days of media hype, trial by television and the radio phone-in, confidence and ability in front of the media's cameras and microphones have become extremely valuable assets for the aspiring manager, and for the person already at the top.

Since natural ability in this medium is rare, the techniques must be learned, and the good PR practitioner should be adept at passing on tips to both the upwardly mobile and established manager alike.

What should be remembered from the outset is that the electronic media are there for you to use, to talk about your factory, your profession, your business or whatever. It is 'free' publicity, and when you consider the sky-high costs of television commercials, especially at peak viewing times, an interview, which costs you nothing but your time, must be infinitely better value.

Even if the media wants to talk to you because something has gone wrong in your company or business, you can nearly always turn that bad news into good news, just as long as you know what you are doing.

But broadcasting is not plain sailing. You must realise, for instance, that the interviewer's aim for an interview and yours are not necessarily – indeed are seldom – the same. The former's objective is to create interesting television, while yours is to get your message across, which means that to achieve your aim you must make your message good television or radio.

Remember you are both using the same article, and the shortage of time is your biggest problem: you will never have enough time when you are being interviewed.

On television, the average interview lasts 2–4 minutes, and for a minute of that the interviewer is talking, so you will have about 90 seconds to tell your story or get your message across. Even if you are interviewed for half an hour the chances are that only a couple of minutes of it will be broadcast; the rest will be edited out.

You should remember what to do when the telephone rings and you are invited to appear, because if your immediate reaction is to think 'I've made it. I'm going to be famous!' and to call your friends on the strength of this to tell them to watch or listen, you could be making a big mistake.

So what are the important points to bear in mind about media interview techniques? The first thing is to make the most of the limited time at your disposal, because the basic premise for giving an interview on television or radio is that it is about saying what you've gone there to say … it is not a courtroom cross-examination and therefore you are under no obligation to go along with the interviewer's line of questioning.

It goes without saying that you must find out, either directly or through your PR consultant, what you are letting yourself in for; often it is your only chance to avoid becoming involved in something very unhelpful, such as a programme which turns out to be anti the business you represent. Unless you ask in advance you could find that you and your company are used as the prime examples, simply because you agreed to take part. You need to ask a lot of questions before you accept an invitation to broadcast.

You also need to remember that 90 per cent of the work of an interview takes place before you leave your office, which means taking time to prepare your message, with PR assistance, and reduce it to something you can say in 90 seconds.

As well as deciding on what you are going to say, you have also to decide what you are not going to say, because there are bound to be subjects you do not want to discuss on air.

Furthermore, if there is a skeleton lurking in your cupboard you have to assume the interviewer knows about it. You must, therefore, be quite clear in your mind what you are going to do if it is brought up – which in most cases means changing the subject! Watch and study politicians when asked direct questions. They seldom answer the question posed, especially if it is a 'difficult' one (in other words, one they prefer not to answer), but they turn the question round to answer an unspoken one they are prepared to answer.

It is not only the aggressive interviewer who can give you a problem – uninformed interviewers, of which alas there are many, are just as dangerous, because silly questions can provoke silly answers if you are not careful.

To broadcast successfully, you have to apply four basic rules: keep it simple, make it personal, quote examples and describe things visually.

The best communicators often use analogies to illustrate significant points. Labour politician Dennis Healey, interviewed on breakfast television talking about the EEC's refusal to impose sanctions on South Africa, said: 'The Danish Prime Minister complained the motion had been amputated. It was more than amputated; in the morning Chancellor Kohl cut off the arms and legs and in the afternoon Mrs Thatcher kicked the torso in the teeth!' He painted a vivid picture of the destruction of an ideal which sticks in the memory.

There are, of course, numerous occasions when you may be called upon to give an interview on radio or television:

- To answer a complaint or query from a member of the public on a live radio phone-in programme.

- To give information on a matter involving your company or organisation on a news or current affairs programme.

- To join a discussion group on a subject which concerns or affects your company or industry, perhaps on a current affairs programme.

CHECKLIST: EFFECTIVE INTERVIEW TECHNIQUES

Here, then, is a list of hints and tips to help you get the most out of a radio or television interview:

- Don't be scared – be prepared. When invited to appear, *ask* and note down:
  - Who's calling; the company; phone number; subject; programme; interviewer; when?; where?; is it live?
  - Why me/us?
  - Who else is involved?
  - Will they be showing any visuals?
  - Most important of all: give yourself time to think before accepting.
- Prepare:
  - Your message: three points maximum, reduced to simple statements. Never write down your answers word-for-word and read them; you are holding a conversation with an interviewer, not reading a statement.

- Your response to all difficult questions.

- Your change-of-direction phrases to control the course of the interview.

- Don't think about who may be listening. Pretend that you and the interviewer are alone and that what you have to tell them is the most important thing they will have ever heard. After all, you are being interviewed because you have information which they want to hear.

  - When you are speaking, don't talk too quickly. Relax, take your time and speak distinctly. Don't mumble or slur your words.

  - Avoid technical terms, professional jargon and organisation slang. Figures and statistics should be kept to a minimum but if you must use figures, always round them off. Too short an answer may give the impression that you are trying to be too smart. Too long an answer is hard to follow and often becomes boring. Just try to say what you have to say in as clear and concise a manner as possible.

- Try to avoid verbal mannerisms such as 'you know', 'at this point in time', 'well, I believe', and 'and so on'.

- At the interview you will always be short of time, so ensure you:

  - Make your point(s) at the beginning.

  - Stick to your own subject. Don't waste time on digressions.

  - Jump on untruths. Interrupt if necessary.

  - Are positive throughout.

  - Mention your company or product (if appropriate) at the beginning, middle and end so that if the interview is cut your product still stands a chance of being referred to.

- Never say: 'No comment. I am unable to confirm or deny.' This often makes it appear that you are confirming whatever it is that the interviewer is asking you. Instead it is better to try variations of 'A full investigation is taking place … ' or 'I don't yet know but … '. After you have effectively said 'No comment' you can then say what you want to say. Be careful about appearing to avoid a question. If you are really on the spot it is probably best to be honest and say you don't know.

- If you are answering a question 'live', that is directly 'on air', do not be afraid to pause and think before you speak. Do not panic if you become tongue-tied or if the interviewer is giving you a difficult time; just take a deep breath and try to remain cool. If it is possible, have a brief chat with the interviewer before you actually start recording so that you have some idea of what questions are likely to be asked.

- Never lose your temper, shout or be rude. Always remain polite and calm, but don't allow yourself to be intimidated by an overbearing interviewer or fellow interviewee.

- If you are being interviewed face-to-face in your own office, make sure you are comfortable. Sit where you want to sit unless it is necessary to move for technical reasons.

- Don't grab hold of the microphone when you are talking. The interviewer or sound recordist will make sure it is in the best position for your voice.

- If the interview is pre-recorded, by all means ask to have it played back. If you are not satisfied you can ask to do all, or part of it, again. If you don't think you can improve on the first effort then just leave it. This, of course, is in an ideal world. My advice is that once you have recorded the interview, it is highly unlikely that an interviewer would agree to do it all over again – unless *all* parties agreed that it was best to do so.

- In order to put across your message effectively, you must:

  - Keep it simple and jargon free.

  - Make it personal, by using personal pronouns.

  - Make it interesting by giving examples.

  - Make it memorable by describing things visually and using analogies.

- There is nothing to be nervous about, unless you have something to hide. In that case it would perhaps be better not to give an interview. Many people are more nervous about giving a radio interview than talking to a reporter with a notebook; in fact, you are in more danger of being misquoted by someone who has to read back his notes than by a microphone which you have actually spoken into.

INTERVIEW TRAINING

Remember, the electronic media is there to be used, and you should be out there using it. But remember, too, that only fools rush in where angels fear to tread. So first find out how to do it.

There are a number of courses available. These can be conducted either internally, aimed at senior executives and run by a professional radio and television interviewer, or at public courses which can attract up to 60 delegates.

Almost all of the well-known radio or TV broadcasters are available – at a price – to undertake detailed sessions for companies. Most popular are people like Peter Hobday, co-presenter of BBC Radio 4's 'Today' pro-gramme, and Douglas Cameron of the London independent station LBC, who is particularly good at giving an insight into the workings of local radio.

For senior executives, a private course for a select few to minimise embar-rassment is recommended. All courses include television equipment, cam-eras and playback facilities.

The private tuition on the successful handling of radio and TV interviews is not cheap, but an effective three-minute interview given by your marketing director can be invaluable to the sales of a product.

Finally, take heart. As Peter Hobday says: 'We do not want a frightened incoherent chief executive on our programmes. It is not our intention to embarrass him, so if he is positive, confident, knows his facts and can respond to us succinctly, then that makes our programme interesting.'

10 PR *on a small budget*

In PR, as in most other things, as I said earlier, you get what you pay for. A PR budget of only £5,000 a year, for instance, certainly won't go very far: it will not cover the cost of engaging the services of a full-time secretary, let alone a skilled PR practitioner, whereas companies with £30,000+ to spend can expect a good degree of professional PR expertise for their money.

But even if budget restrictions do not allow you to employ an in-house PR professional or an outside consultancy, you can still make use of PR techniques to promote your company, association or product, whether it be a small hotel or a national charity.

Tips on how to do so are scattered throughout this book. However, since I realise that many companies and organisations face the dilemma of wanting to operate PR but with very small funds at their disposal, here are some basic steps. To make the guidelines more relevant, the requirements of a small, town-centre hotel are used as an illustration, but of course most of the principles can be applied to most service sectors, such as retail outlets, and can be adapted by small businesses of various descriptions.

THE HOTEL SCENARIO

Know your market

It is absolutely no use trying to implement a PR plan unless you know the market for which you are catering and the market you are out to satisfy. If your hotel is patronised almost exclusively by travelling salespeople, and you are quite happy to stay with this market but would like to expand it further, there would be no point promoting your hotel extensively within the immediate neighbourhood. Instead, the PR effort should be directed at the travelling salespeople who do not already know of your hotel's existence and the facilities it can offer them.

This can be done through magazines devoted to the sales and marketing sectors of the community, and through the business/commerce columns of national newspapers.

It could well be, on the other hand, that while occupancy rates at your hotel during the week are excellent, the place practically 'dies' at the weekends when the business guests are not around. In this case you either need to encourage business guests to stay on over the weekend, either by introducing low-price weekend breaks, or attract the leisure market to fill the empty rooms from Friday to Monday.

Why your product?

Once you have established the market you want your PR to reach, it is important to appraise your product honestly, and determine its strengths and weaknesses – in particular any *unique selling points* (USPs). Very few aspects of life, of course, are unique, but if you take a good, long look at your product you should be able to come up with some plus points that distinguish it from the competition.

Talk to your regular guests, and find out from them why they prefer using your hotel to the one down the road.

Is it, for example, because your room rates are lower than the competition's, your bar is the liveliest in town, the facilities you offer the business guest are particularly good (specific writing surfaces in bedrooms, together with trouser presses, tea/coffee making facilities and the like), or is your restaurant far and away the best locally?

Whatever the reasons, once you have established them you are well on the way to being able to instigate a PR action plan.

PR action plan

Having determined the market you are seeking and the USPs you believe should do the trick, make yourself familiar with the media which could be useful to you, whether it be business press, sales/marketing magazines, local radio, women's magazines or whatever. The reference section of your local library should have directories giving not only complete listings of the media but circulation figures, copy deadlines and the like; there are also specialist directories available.

Step two is to create a PR angle that is likely to interest the targeted media, based on your hotel's USPs. If, for example, the best thing about your hotel is its restaurant, in which you are employing, at vast expense, a very bright and innovative young chef, your target media will be not only your local newspapers and radio stations, to encourage more local diners, but also specialist food writers from the national media, particularly the up-market magazines. Getting your restaurant mentioned in a publication such as *Vogue*, *Harper's & Queen* or one of the credit card companies' glossies such as Diner's Club's *Signature* can ensure its success for years.

So how do you create a PR angle that might interest the media in your restaurant? Simply inviting a representative of the target media to come and sample a meal is not enough; indeed, since food writers are inundated with invitations to try the thousands of new restaurants constantly springing up in all parts of the country, an invitation from you, unless given the PR treatment, is quite likely to fall by the wayside.

The answer is to make the restaurant seem excitingly different, either in ambience or food or, preferably, both. If it specialises in English food, for example, get the chef to introduce a range of unusual dishes culled from an ancient recipe book, or dishes which are peculiar to the area in which your hotel is located. In other words, be creative and innovative about the aspects of your product you believe are worth highlighting, and you stand a much better chance of enticing the media, if for no other reason than that the ancient recipes of unusual dishes will give the journalist an angle for his/her story.

The above is a very simple example of basic PR which can be achieved at very little cost, except in time. And the same basic principles apply whatever is being marketed or promoted.

PR done skilfully is an expensive and time-consuming practice, but one which can, and does, produce excellent results. There is absolutely no reason that the basic PR principles cannot be applied by small businesses which simply do not have the money.

The writing of a press release, for example, is an acquired skill, and badly written ones can do more harm than good. Engaging the services of a local freelance journalist to write them on your behalf is a sensible option. He or she may even waive a cash fee for the exercise in return for a couple of elaborate meals in your restaurant!

There is no great myth or mystique to public relations – it is basically a matter of common sense, doing your homework, and then being realistic about what you hope to achieve, and how you are going to achieve it.

11 *New product launches*

The same basic guidelines apply no matter what you are launching, whether it be a restaurant, a magazine or a new car.

LAUNCH THEME AND DATE

Decide on a theme for the launch. This could involve a special venue, date, number, colour, dish, costume etc. It could also mean having to hire special equipment or book personalities. But remember that the media are interested in a *story*, so do not go to great lengths for a theme for the media and forget to create an interesting, newsworthy story for them.

What deciding on a date for the launch, ensure that:

- The chief executives of the company will be available.

- The date does not clash with a similar launch or other major media event.

- The most important media representatives are likely to attend.

Obviously no date will suit everyone, so after taking the above precautions it is best to settle on a date as soon as possible.

VENUE

Make sure:

- The cost of the venue is within the company's budget.

- It is a reasonable size for the number of people you expect to attend.

- That, if at all possible, it is in a central location convenient for the majority of the guests.

REFRESHMENTS

- Decide whether a meal or refreshments will be offered, and who will provide them.

- Give caterers an indication of numbers. (These can be finalised nearer the time of the event.)

GUEST LIST AND INVITATIONS

- Invite all media who are likely to be interested in the launch, not just the obvious ones.

- Try finding out the names of specific journalists in advance to avoid having to address invitations to the editor, the news editor, etc.

- Produce printed invitations to be sent out, if possible, three weeks in advance.

- After a week to ten days, telephone those who have not replied and compile a list of acceptances.

- On the day before the event, telephone all invitees as a final reminder.

PHOTOGRAPHY

- Book a photographer to take both colour and black-and-white pictures of the launch which can be offered to the media.

CLIENT BRIEFING

- Make sure that the client or chief executive knows exactly what is going to happen on the day of the event: who will be speaking, who will deal with questions from the floor, etc.

PRESS KITS

- Compile press kits for the event that include all pertinent information about the launch, together with any appropriate photographs.

- Make sure a press kit is sent as soon as possible to any relevant media who are not able to attend the event.

- Ensure your telephone number is included in the press kit so that you can be contacted after the event for additional information.

SPECIAL MEDIA REQUIREMENTS

- If radio and television representatives are expected, discuss in advance of the event the facilities they require and the timing of the interviews.

- Try to 'pre-sell' exclusive story angles to a variety of publications and media in advance of the launch.

12 *Crisis public relations: How to handle emergencies*

THE GUIDELINES

The major part of this chapter has been written by Doug Goodman, Managing Director of Doug Goodman Public Relations and former head of PR for Britain's largest holiday company. He writes on how you should prepare and cope with an emergency, shows how good planning pays dividends and offers some useful case studies. But first we consider some general principles.

Not all that a public relations officer touches results in favourable coverage. If only that could be the case! So, what should be done about unfavourable coverage or in the event of an emergency?

PR practitioners naturally endeavour to ensure that every piece of coverage is favourable. But though they may succeed in getting the media to visit a particular restaurant, a tv crew into a particular hotel, the city editor to meet a particular chief executive, or a specific editor to visit a particular factory, there is no guarantee that coverage will result from the exercise, or that, if it does, it will be favourable. A good PRO will do everything to ensure that all the arrangements go smoothly, that everyone is briefed, and that the 'positive', favourable facts and angles are presented. But at the end of the day – and this is the big difference between advertising and PR – even with the most professional PR assistance, one is ultimately in the hands of the media.

Generally speaking, if unfavourable coverage does result the best advice is to forget about it, and move on to the next exercise, unless, that is, the piece of coverage is by a majority vote positively unfair and damaging, when an approach to the editor/news editor is in order or, in the final analysis, to one's lawyers. Making a fuss at other times is unlikely to achieve anything except frayed tempers.

When there *has* been an emergency, such as a fire, death or any other major disaster within your organisation, it is advisable to follow a set rule of procedures in order to try to ensure that the incident is portrayed accurately and fairly to the media.

Any of the above events could result in headline news in your area and possibly even nationally, so it is important to realise that special steps should be taken to ensure that the company or organisation's point of view is represented and that any questions are handled with the organisation's best interests in mind. If the PRO is not on duty then the most senior person should assume the following responsibilities:

- Before attempting to make statements to the media, the PRO designate must instruct all staff and personnel that no one other than the appointed spokesperson or team is to communicate with or answer questions from the media or public. All enquiries should be channelled through the spokesperson in order that replies are consistent.

- Take the names, addresses, telephone numbers and fax numbers of the media who have contacted you. Also note the time they rang and any deadlines they have to meet.

- Make sure home telephone numbers of individual management representatives are kept on file in order that you can communicate with them out of office hours.

- The PRO designate must take control and should tell the media that a representative of the organisation will phone back as soon as possible; he or she must never appear to be negative and should always assume an authoritative attitude.

- Develop a statement that clarifies the organisation's position. Discuss this with the police if they are involved; invariably they will also be preparing a press statement at the same time.

- If death, injury or accident have occurred, you should never release names or addresses of those involved without first checking with the police to ensure that the next-of-kin have been informed. And it's usually wise to let the authorities make the notification as they are trained in the required skills.

- Read your statement to the press and avoid being drawn into further discussions unless you are clear what your reply will be.

- In most circumstances, an initial statement such as 'we are investigating the incident' will suffice until a more detailed response has been researched and prepared.

CRISIS PR IN PRACTICE

Doug Goodman, Managing Director of Doug Goodman Public Relations:

Stop and think about the worst possible situation that could occur in your organisation. As an in-house PR executive or a consultant, what sort of crisis or problems are you likely to be called on to handle?

Think back over the recent past to the tragedies which have hit the headlines all too frequently and perhaps offer a silent word of sympathy to the PR practitioners and other members of organisations who have had to resolve many varied problems and maintain the good name of their company.

PR can only be one of many tools employed in the problem-solving business: a good management team, adequate communications, security and administration groups and staff or customer welfare teams must all play a role. And most fundamental of all must be a company policy of caring about people, of putting welfare and safety before profit. A company which has sloppy procedure or an attitude of not caring about the customer will inevitably be exposed.

All too often company management decides to call in the PRO as the disaster unfolds and expects the PR expert to take the pain away. Just as you cannot learn to give a good TV interview as you head towards the studio, public relations cannot solve a problem when it is brought in too late.

The right place for PR is at the top, reporting to the managing director or a very senior person. The PR executive must guide and advise, must know about everything happening in the company or in the client's organisation and, most important of all, he or she must anticipate.

A key role for PR is to work closely with senior company staff to devise and implement a plan for handling disasters. Any company not prepared for a small problem or a major disaster is inviting trouble.

What do we mean by a disaster? Think back again over the past year or two and try to recall some of the headline-hitting stories. Some will have occurred where no possible blame can be attached to the organisation, others will have been caused by rules being broken or poor working practices.

In Britain in recent years there have been air, rail and sea disasters – notably the Townsend Thoresen ferry tragedy and the Thames pleasureboat sinking, oil rig incidents, sabotage of supermarket products including the Perrier problem and many others. What all these have in common is that customers' safety and welfare were at stake and that the image of the organisations would suffer if the correct action was not taken. It is all too easy to decide in retrospect what the action should have been and how the outcome might have been different.

But if a company comes out of a disaster with its reputation destroyed, its customer confidence lost and its staff morale in shreds, then quite clearly something went wrong! So can PR prevent things 'going wrong'? Yes, in certain circumstances it certainly can and should be involved in the planning of appropriate procedures and courses of action for dealing with disasters. PR should also be involved in the training of key people and the rehearsal of scenarios; in the counselling and advising during an incident; in damage limitation or turning potentially bad news into the positive; and in evaluation and discussion after the event.

While a large company may have further to fall than a small one if it mishandles a problem, the small one needs to be just as adequately prepared. Big organisations can devote the resources to disaster management more readily than the smaller companies so there may be a need to investigate the use of specialist PR consultancies that can be called on to advise and help.

One large organisation which takes disaster management very seriously is Thomson Tour Operations, the UK's biggest tour operator. Part of the Thomson Travel Group, which controls Britannia Airways, Lunn Poly and Portland Holidays, Thomson Tour Operations carries about three million holiday-makers abroad annually. Using the Boeing jets of Britannia, other charter and scheduled airlines, the tour operator offers a year-round programme of inclusive holidays from up to 16 UK airports to over 50 countries from Bali to Bermuda and Siberia to the Seychelles. In summer 100 charter flights each week carry Thomson clients to Mallorca alone. Up to 200,000 people are on holiday with the company at any one time and nearly 2,000 staff are based overseas to ensure that the holidays run smoothly.

With so many clients spread around the world it is inevitable that when incidents like terrorist activities, health problems, strikes, natural disasters and others occur, they will become involved.

And it is a philosophy based on care of the client and quality of service which ensures that Thomson has the resources and experience to deal with problems. While some organisations believe it could never happen to them, at Thomson the belief is 'not if, but when'.

Highly experienced specialist teams are available in the company with resources which expand to match any need. At the company's head office in London a permanently staffed operations centre with a very sophisticated information and communications network is at the heart of the system. Key people who can assemble special teams at very short notice are on permanent call and precisely defined procedures ensure that everyone knows his/her role.

While PR would have a very high profile during the handling of an incident it is successful teamwork which stands out.

The leisure business in general is very newsworthy and holidays in particular provide a vast amount of material for the media. Most of the time the press coverage is good but when problems occur on holiday the press is quick to report the events. It is a sad fact of life that one Briton mugged in Spain will gain more column centimetres than a natural disaster affecting thousands of people in the Far East.

The media is generally very fair and I can recall very few occasions during my time as head of PR when the media failed to request and publish a company spokesperson's comments at the end of a critical item. It is vital therefore that adequately trained staff can always be contacted by the press.

It is the PRO's specific responsibility to ensure that staff are available every minute of the day and night, are fully briefed on current events, are aware of company policy and an agreed statement and are trained to deal with anything from a peak-time television news interview downward. The release of information to the press must be strictly controlled as only a few key people are permitted to make a comment.

Much emphasis is placed on short- and long-term preparation and practice. Regular radio and TV familiarisation courses are held in order to give management the opportunity to go through the very worst situations which could be encountered.

The up-sides and down-sides of every problem are written down and analysed, while role-playing helps define the key points which the company spokesman must make.

Rehearsal is of tremendous value. This was proved when BBC Radio 4 wanted an early morning comment from the company on how the latest Basque bombing campaign in Spain was likely to affect tourism. The very same questions had been rehearsed the previous evening.

As part of its disaster management plan, Thomson holds exercises where various groups participate, at very short notice, in major incidents. Strengths and weakness can be pinpointed and procedures improved. On one occasion 50 people took part in a simulated coach crash. The PR department played a prominent role as, unknown to them and the directors, a press conference had to be arranged at ten minutes' notice for national press, radio and TV who arrived at the company's head office.

The head of PR had been 'written out' of the day's exercise and was able to muster an army of extras as well as a professional film unit to take the parts of very demanding press people. The final version of the film, which was edited and presented like a TV news item, showed up a number of deficiencies. For example, the 'press' had not been prevented from interviewing 'bereaved' clients; insufficient control of the press conference was apparent; company spokespeople gave conflicting statements.

As a result of the rehearsals and regular group discussions, methods of disaster management are being constantly refined and updated.

A major concern in the PR group is always whether sufficient of them would be available at the time of an incident. With foreign travel taking up a large part of the members' time, some of the executives could be absent at any given moment.

The first two hours after an incident are crucial in press-relations terms. During that time the PR team must assemble, establish policy, prepare and issue a statement and an emergency phone number, brief the company spokesperson and prepare for several hundred telephone and face-to-face interviews.

Previous experience has shown how vital it is to take the initiative and act, rather than react, during these first few hours.

It is unlikely that a disaster will unfold at a convenient 10.30 am on a Tuesday and be resolved by the end of the day. It will happen at the worst possible time. To overcome the concern at having insufficient PR resources, a back-up team of 12 could be summoned to run a press information centre.

The press's needs tend to unfold in a predictable way: the Press Association and the national papers, radio and TV get the news within 20 minutes, the provincials call within two hours and the weekly papers make contact two days later asking if anyone from their area was involved.

Good and extensive contacts within the media are of such fundamental importance to the PR practitioner that the point needs no stressing. Tip-offs and advance warning from the press about incidents can assist the PRO greatly.

In one incident, a senior journalist phoned to advise the PRO that reports had just been received of an aircraft crash in the Canary Islands. No other details were available but the journalist would call back exactly two minutes later to check whether it was an aircraft chartered by Thomson. That professional kindness enabled the PR head and operations team to check that all company flights were safe and to establish that, tragically, one operator's aircraft was indeed missing. When the return call came two minutes later, closely followed by dozens of others, adequate resources were in place to give accurate information immediately.

In an average week the press and PR team at Thomson Tour Operations will handle several hundred press enquiries. The vast majority of these written and telephoned requests are of a routine nature but several will concern holiday problems. Most problems arise through an event which is entirely beyond the control of the company. An illness, accident or death has occurred and the press wants to know what action has been taken. Strikes or terrorist activity may disrupt holiday arrangements and again the press requires information on how the company is handling the situation and looking after the welfare of its clients.

On the rare occasion when the press follows up a story where a client has complained about accommodation being below standard, building work or service of a low quality, the company may well be at fault. Not only must accurate information be given to the press but the situation must be fully investigated to ensure that, if necessary, things are put right.

But what both types of problem have in common is that they require prompt, accurate and honest answers: prompt because newspapers have deadlines and if information is needed in 20 minutes then after lunch will not be acceptable; accurate and honest because if you lie you will be caught out and no one will ever trust you again.

Being accurate and honest does not mean always divulging everything. When a client books a holiday with Thomson, a confidential contract is made so such details as names and addresses will not be released to any-body – except when the police request it. This rule naturally applies to press requests for client information and, however demanding these requests become, the rule is not broken. This is a very sensitive area and must be handled with care.

On many occasions a problem which might have resulted in adverse press coverage has been turned to the company's advantage. Holiday-makers hospitalised overseas or repatriation by air ambulance have provided good human-angled stories which had a happy ending through the care and concern shown by company staff.

'John praises holiday reps', says one headline. 'Their staff were wonderful and did everything to help us', a couple were reported as saying after a robbery. 'Thanks to prompt action by Thomson staff our daughter got the best medical treatment possible', another paper said after an accident in Greece.

Nothing spectacular, you might think. Staff were only doing their job. Nevertheless it is gratifying to see a potentially critical story turned to one which demonstrates genuine care for the customer.

The value of good communications was demonstrated when a terrorist bomb destroyed a parked aircraft in Sri Lanka. The Thomson representative advised the company operations department who in turn called the press officers at home to tell them that the four passengers on the programme were safe and wished to continue their holiday.

When the press called for a comment the company spokesperson was able to respond at once with the details. So efficient are the overseas staff and operations personnel that the press offices are often called late at night with information about what might seem fairly trivial accidents or incidents. But it is better to have too much information than none whatsoever.

To ensure that a company spokesperson is always available the press office is staffed from 8.00 am to 7.00 pm, and during evenings and at weekends radio pagers and mobile phones are used.

The world's worst nuclear disaster – the Chernobyl power station explosion – tested Thomson to the full. The company operates a year-round programme of holidays to the USSR and at the end of April 1986 it had 274 clients in Moscow and Leningrad. From the time the news arrived in the West until their clients were brought home, staff experienced the five most intensive days for many years.

Teamwork was the key to the success of the operation and while a fairly small number of people were directly involved, many more contributed. A video film was made by the company some weeks after the event and the teamwork was reconstructed to show others in the company exactly how disaster management plans had worked.

Although there were no Thomson clients in Kiev, the nearest tourist city to Chernobyl, Moscow was only 400 miles distant. As the size of the disaster became known and reports suggested that radioactive clouds were drifting eastwards, Thomson sought assurances from the USSR and from British nuclear specialists. Nobody was prepared to state that no risk existed so under company policy, which puts health and safety before all other considerations, guests and staff would have to be brought home.

The first phone call to the company's office in Moscow drew comments about the weather. News of the seriousness of the situation had not yet reached them. Letters were prepared for the clients in Moscow and Leningrad advising them of the situation and plans were made to send an aircraft to bring them home.

By this time the Western press was carrying headlines like 'thousands dead' and 'nuke hole of death' and interest was focusing on Britons 'stranded in the USSR'.

A statement was issued to the effect that all tours to the USSR had been suspended by Thomson and the news was carried by BBC TV. The press office worked at full stretch issuing bulletins and answering questions. The operations department investigated the many and varied methods of 'rescue'. The client welfare department handled large numbers of calls from worried relatives and friends of those on holiday in the USSR.

The continental department took the key role of maintaining communications with Moscow. This involved keeping a phone line open for several days and using it without a break. The phone bill came to over £4,000.

To arrange a special flight over Soviet territory takes weeks under normal conditions. Every hour was critical. The Foreign Office in London was asked for help and diplomatic staff in Moscow tried to speed up formalities. The first day of May arrived and on May Day the Soviet Union closes for national celebrations. The aircraft, which had been standing by, was required elsewhere. The first day of the company's summer programme began, putting more pressure on the operations department.

A growing volume of press questions were asking what the tour operator was doing to bring its passengers home. Just after midday on 1 May official permission was granted.

A further complication had arisen before departure on the ten-hour round-trip. Radiation-detection equipment set up at Heathrow to screen arriving passengers was not to be made available. Detection equipment had to be put on the aircraft and letters of advice on health checks written and distributed to passengers.

The home landing was schedule for 6.00 am at Gatwick and the focus of the press turned to the arrival of the first package tourists from Russia. The company had to consider whether its clients would wish to be greeted by the media. The Thomson press team announced that senior staff and representatives, who had been working in the USSR, would be available at a press conference at the airport.

As the first returning clients, accompanied by Thomson staff in full uniform, came through the barrier, cameras closed in and the press began their interviews. Comments were positive and the company was praised for its action and concern shown by staff.

At 8.00 am on 'Breakfast TV News', the report from Gatwick ended with Doug Goodman saying that his company's first priority was always the safety and comfort of its holiday-makers. A carefully prepared plan and professional approach had ensured that a potentially damaging situation was turned to the company's advantage.

CONCLUSION

By now the importance of the right philosophy must be apparent and adopting the attitude of 'it can't happen to us' is inviting disaster.

The key points for the PR executive or the consultant called in by a client are these:

- Anticipation.
- Preparation.
- Action.

All the possible incidents and disasters must be anticipated and their effect on the company analysed. The preparation must include the written production of a disaster manual, the selection and training of staff to deal with different aspects of the event, particularly media handling, and a rehearsal of the groups of people involved. When disaster does strike, the carefully prepared procedures will ensure that the event is handled with a professional and caring attitude.

13 Case history I: The Chief Executive's approach to PR

INTRODUCTION

When I took on my current role as Chief Executive I had no direct experience of public relations, but was obliged to acquire some quickly. Quite apart from the fact that suddenly various people from the media wanted to talk to me and ask my opinion on industry-related matters, I was somewhat dismayed that every time I picked up the many trade journals or magazines, our principal competitor seemed to be getting a lot of coverage. It was apparent that when it came to PR, they were trying harder.

I therefore undertook to establish a serious PR effort.

The experts tell us that 'PR is a means of projecting the desired image of one's company and products with a view to enhancing sales', or words to that effect.

That it may be, but when I took up the reins I regarded the whole area as a minefield of voracious reporters of whom I was terrified, since I was convinced they were waiting to catch me out and publicly demonstrate how little I knew about my industry in general and my own company and products in particular.

I also had a somewhat jaundiced view of the value of public relations, since my experience had been restricted to being presented with expenses for lavish entertainment or sponsored events, which appeared to be nothing more than a 'jolly' for management, the justification invariably being 'But this is a good public relations exercise'.

THE VALUE OF PR

In the light of subsequent experience, however, I now regard public relations as an indispensable ingredient in the marketing mix. Correctly planned and executed, it is a uniquely powerful method of cost-effectively communicating an image of your company to target audiences which cannot be achieved through direct sales and/or advertising.

Now I know there is a school of thought that labels PR as 'just free advertising'. I would urge readers not to be misled. We all know that nothing is free, and public relations is no exception. But to my mind public relations and advertising are quite separate and distinct. Obviously each of the elements in marketing has a role to play, but where PR has a definite advantage in a media context is that the message is highly credible.

While advertising is controllable, in that it enables us to select an attention-grabbing headline and to ensure that the copy spells out the product benefits, the readers of that advertisement are aware that they are being told what you want them to know. By contrast, if consumers read an ostensibly independent editorial, they are far more likely to believe its contents and to give it credence.

There is an old adage that word-of-mouth advertising is the best advertising. The value is undisputed. Word-of-mouth advertising is actually public relations at its best. The reason it works so well is that the message is 'independent' and therefore highly credible.

If one accepts that public relations can be a real asset, the decision then is how to use it to best effect. Who is the target audience and what is it that you want them to believe of you? The target audience is, of course, particular to each industry and the job to be done.

Public relations gives the capacity to create awareness of your company and products, depending on the frequency with which your messages appear; it can be used to project a desirable image of your company and products, or indeed to correct an image deficiency.

Whether you opt for a strategic or a tactical route or a combination of both, and whether you use public relations to talk to your consumers, to your own staff, or to lobby government or other centres of influence, must be your decision according to your company's needs.

Whatever your goals or objectives, public relations can play a key role if it is well planned and executed. Like all seemingly simple things, however, my experience has been that it is quite difficult to achieve. So let me explain the process that we went through to establish a meaningful PR effort.

GUIDELINES FOR CHOOSING A PR COMPANY

In our case we felt that we were being out-performed in PR terms within the travel trade. Travel agents are a major source of business to us and our principal competitor had historically had the lion's share of this business. Furthermore, we were aware that they were perceived to be better in tune with the needs of the travel industry.

We viewed the travel trade, therefore, as our key target for PR effort. We were convinced that our product and service levels were as good as, if not better than, those of the competition, but the travel trade had a different perception. The task was one of image correction, plus maximising awareness of our products and services in order to enhance bookings.

So we elected to appoint a PR company to drive this effort. That is where the problems began. Not, I hasten to add, in deciding to appoint a PR consultant, but in our choice of company.

We invited six consultancies to put forward their ideas of how we could achieve our objectives through PR, and a number of considerations emerged in making that choice. There are the fairly obvious ones of cost and of industry knowledge, the latter being particularly important, since knowledge of one's own industry suggests that the PR company concerned should have well-established contacts with the appropriate media and understand the nature of the business in which you are engaged. A good indicator of industry knowledge is to take a look at the client list of a PR company to see whether they have an existing client company from within your own industry or allied industries.

The third factor is the content and quality of the presentation that is made to you by each company. Obviously one expects it to be professional, to demonstrate an empathy for your needs and to convince you that the company is capable of creating solutions, backed up by a pragmatic approach to implementing proposals.

These elements are pretty obvious and quite tangible, but there are also intangibles that are worth considering. If there is a stunningly attractive person making the presentation, this can cloud one's objectivity and must be guarded against, while at the other end of the scale one has to allow that, while seeking a high level of professionalism, even the most experienced presenters may be nervous when pitching for your business.

There are also, to my mind, a couple of less obvious pitfalls in the selection process. The first is to establish who will run the account.

We experienced a number of instances where the presentations were extremely professional and very convincing, but it quickly became apparent that the 'heavyweight' team had been sent in to make the presentation to us, and that they were not likely to have very much to do with running the account. My advice would be to insist that one deals at the time of presentation with the individual or individuals who are going to be in charge of your account.

Another major pitfall is in establishing that the consultant you prefer is actually sufficiently adaptable to your industry's needs. In any service industry we have to be prepared to be all things to all people, which requires a degree of flexibility, something that may not suit the operating style of every PR agency.

The third, and to my mind the most important, pitfall to avoid is failing to recognise that you will be working very closely with whoever runs your account. As such, it is crucial that the 'chemistry' is right and that you actually feel you can work effectively together. My recommendation would be to view the whole process on very similar lines to that of selecting a key employee for your company. Having established that the basic qualifications for the position are acceptable, it is critical to ensure that that person will fit in as part of your team in order that they can make the maximum contribution to your company's goals.

At the time we were making our selection of a PR company, we did not have the wisdom of hindsight. We selected a company with an excellent track record and were influenced by the fact that they had as one of their clients another company in our group, which spoke very highly of their performance. There was great goodwill, many exchanges of good ideas, and we felt that our PR effort was about to unleash itself upon the marketplace.

It became apparent, however, after some while that we had a real problem. We seemed to be doing an enormous amount of planning and so on, but we were not seeing any – or, at least, not many – tangible results. We worried away at this for some months and finally came to the conclusion that we had made a dreadful mistake and appointed the wrong company.

We decided, therefore, to cut our losses and to start again with the whole process of briefing and selecting a new agency. Obviously this is a time consuming process and it is galling to admit that one had made such a bad error of judgement, so we were at some pains to try to analyse what had gone wrong. We realised that there were a number of factors involved, but it was by no means all the agency's fault.

In our naïvety in this whole field we had assumed that, having appointed and briefed an agency, the professionals would then take over and get the job done. What we had not realised is that, unlike external consultants in many other areas of business, with public relations it has to be a totally interactive process. To achieve that successfully one has to have the correct internal set-up to feed the agency with sufficient good quality material to enable them to use their professionalism to best effect.

The agency also needs to have a central point of contact to deal with the myriad enquiries and queries that emerge, and they have to have your time to obtain the necessary approvals, comments, quotations etc, in order that they can get on and do the job effectively. I think we had not appreciated how critical it is to establish the internal set-up correctly in order to get the most out of a PR consultancy relationship. The other fact that became apparent was that in this case the agency we had selected had very limited industry knowledge and contacts and therefore was unable to get the maximum impact from the material they were being given.

It was a painful lesson and an expensive one.

INTERNAL SYSTEMS

Before appointing a new PR company we established a simple but effective internal set-up which operates at three levels. The first point of contact is at our head office, where the marketing services manager is on hand to respond to our PR consultants with requests for information, organising promotional material and so on to be available at the right place at the right time for photographic shots or whatever it may be, and to handle the many requests for information or assistance on a timely basis.

The second and principal point of contact is our marketing director, who liaises directly with the agency account director in agreeing the various actions that need to be undertaken, developing the plans and projects for future PR activity, approving press releases, and generally taking overall responsibility for ensuring that we are on the path to achieving our objectives. The marketing director meets with the agency every fortnight as a matter of routine and as and when required in between.

The third point of contact is myself, and I'm involved whenever we have a policy issue to decide upon or it is felt that my presence or a quotation from me, is likely to be better received by the media. I have a rule of always taking the agency's advice in these instances and try to make myself available whenever they feel it will be of benefit.

On the broader corporate front, of course as part of a world-wide organisation we have an in-house PR director at our European division level. She will feed through items on a world-wide basis for use at country level and generally advise on European PR policy.

So, having selected the right agency for *your* needs and created the right internal structure to meet *their* needs, the next point to consider is the brief to the agency.

BRIEFING THE AGENCY

Obviously, as part of the selection process, we have already covered the overall goals and objectives and target audiences that we are looking to address with the PR effort. I would stress very strongly, however, that it is critical that one does not leave it at this point.

If the PR executives are to get maximum results for you, it is crucial that you take them into your confidence totally and tell them as much as you possibly can about the workings of your business; the opportunities, the problems, your fears and aspirations, the strengths and weaknesses of your organisation and those of your competitors; in other words make them part of your company.

They need to know where they have to be additionally alert, where they can seek opportunities, and above all they have to understand the tenor of the way in which you want to present your image. Ideally, the individuals working on your account should feel part of your organisation and have a complete understanding of all of the business issues. Actually, some of these will be confidential and they will not be able to use them, but if it helps their understanding then, personally, I'm all for it.

It should be recognised as well that this is not a one-off exercise but an on-going process. If your PR company is to be aware of the many opportunities that exist it is critical that it is kept fully up to date on product and service developments, corporate news, any promotional activity that may be going on, current advertising strategy, key personnel changes and so on.

We actually make a point of reviewing our total business strategy with our PR agency, and have found that by all of the account directors understanding their role in our overall strategic plan, they are better equipped to achieve the results we are looking for.

I would also strongly recommend that at a very early stage you agree upon an operating practice which suits both parties. We operate a system of detailed action plans, supplemented with monthly activity reports. This system seems to work very well for us in that both parties are absolutely aware of who is doing what, and when, and we can all see that we are on target, or not, as the case may be. Through the monthly activity reports we then measure the results we have achieved from our efforts.

RESTRICTIONS AND FREEDOM

As the relationship with our PR agency has developed there have been a number of other points that have emerged which I think are worth mentioning.

The first is on the confidentiality of information. We have a corporate policy not to divulge any financial results, and obviously this is a real frustration for the agency.

When the results are good it is a major frustration for me, too, but we obviously cannot buck the corporate policy, and therefore have to find a way round the problem. This particular restriction, however, tends to endorse my philosophy of being totally open with the agency people and involving them completely. I have no problem in their being a party to our financial results so that they can understand we have nothing to hide; this, in turn, enables them to be positive about the company's performance and its prospects without having to divulge sensitive information.

The other factor, for which I am extremely grateful, is that we are blessed with a PR director in our agency who has no qualms about telling me that such-and-such an idea will not work. I would strongly recommend that this is an attitude to be encouraged either internally or from a consultant. We are paying these people as experts and they understand the media. I, for one, would rather not waste all of our time on pursuing something I happen to think is a good idea but the experts tell me 'won't fly'. That, of course, comes back to the elusive element I mentioned in the selection process: chemistry. The chemistry between you and your people and the agency staff working on your account is a crucial factor and I would again recommend fostering the type of rapport that will ensure that you do not waste any time unnecessarily.

TIPS ON CONTROLLING AND MOTIVATING THE PR EFFORT

Having selected your PRO or consultancy, organised your internal set-up and managed the on-going briefing requirement, you could be forgiven for thinking that this is the end of the task.

PR consultants are human, and like all people they need controlling and motivating. To my mind, these two things go hand in hand. I have already explained the controls we exercise through regular personal meetings supported by detailed action plans and activity reports, which give us a comfort level that the required job is being done. They also enable us as managers to recognise a job well done and to address constructively those areas where we feel we could still do more. Since public relations results are to a large extent subjective, I think it is particularly crucial that one has adequate means of recognising good performances and to quantify as far as possible the results of the PR people's effort.

We are totally prepared to take our PR consultants into our confidence, and I know that this is something they appreciate. Above all, I feel it is necessary to take every opportunity to demonstrate that we view our PR consultants as part of the whole team and to that end, whenever we have national sales or branch managers' meetings, we invite our PR consultants along. There is no PR work as such for them to do, but I want them to feel part of the group and to absorb the spirit of the organisation and what we are trying to do. Add to this regular meetings and reviews with senior management, and there is an overt demonstration that we really are committed to the PR exercise and are appreciative of our PR consultant's efforts.

There is, of course, always a sneaking fear that if one is too effusive in praise of a job well done the PR people will see this as a *carte blanche* to ask for more money. But good PROs are professionals, and I have not had cause to review my advice.

Regard your PR agency as part of your staff and do not overlook the fact that, like all people, they will work better if they understand the total picture, their role in it, and see that their efforts are recognised.

AM I GETTING WHAT I EXPECTED?

There is a tendency among people employing PROs to expect not only too much, but also things to happen too quickly. Public relations is a powerful force, but it is a mistake to expect that it will elicit an instant response from the target audiences, whereas advertising may well do that. Public relations is almost by definition a soft sell, and it takes time to build up a momentum of opinion-forming to a point where one actually sees tangible results. Despite these caveats however, the answer to the question 'Am I getting everything I expected to out of the PR effort?' is an unequivocal 'Yes; albeit I still want more'.

We targeted on changing the opinions of the travel trade first and foremost and on maximising awareness of our products and services. We are seeing a 50 per cent increase in our travel agency business, and while I am not suggesting that all of that is attributable to public relations, there is no doubt in my mind that the PR effort has had a significant impact on that result.

Certainly, not everything we have tried has worked; we have had our disappointments and our frustrations. But public relations is now an integral part of our marketing mix and we are a stronger organisation as a result of it.

From a purely personal standpoint, I with many of my colleagues have overcome our fear of dealing with the media, thanks to the support of our PR agency staff, who ensured in the earlier days in particular that they were always in attendance during interviews to help out, to advise, and generally to give moral support.

To summarise, then, in a relatively short period of time I have moved from being something of a cynic when it came to the value of PR to believing that it is potentially a uniquely powerful method of cost-effectively communicating an image for your company to selected audiences; and that, in my opinion, is an asset no company should be without.

14 Case history II: The lobbyist

A day in the life of a lobbyist! What is a lobbyist? What do lobbyists do? Is it a part of PR?

What lobbyists do is called lobbying. It *is* part of the broad world of PR or public affairs. The lobbyist is someone who, on behalf of his client, relates to the world of those in positions of authority and power in politics and government; primarily peers, MPs and senior civil servants. Peers gain their positions of authority either by inheritance or political patronage; MPs are elected by their fellow citizens; civil servants are appointed by the government. All of them have recognised status and authority to take part in the process of government. The lobbyist is a non-elected person of self-created status who is paid to influence those in positions of authority, elected and appointed, so that his particular interest is advanced in such a way that legislation is passed or government management decisions are made that favour the lobbyist's employer.

Not many Britons are deeply interested in the actual, day-to-day working of politics and government power. Most media reporting on the subject is confined to a description of actual events or to gossip about personalities which are of surface interest only. As the lobbyist has to earn his living from knowing the realities of the political world, he has to work hard to be fully informed at all times and across the whole range of British political activity.

Nowadays, the process of government is so complex that the lobbyist has to extend his influence to many persons outside his country's elected representatives to include civil servants, servants of the legislature, local government officials, members of trade unions or trade associations, influential persons in business, commerce and the media and, sometimes, to considerable numbers of ordinary citizens. (I have referred to the lobbyists as 'him' simply for convenience; in fact many of the most effective lobbyists in the UK are women.)

Those who mount a lobby can come from a variety of backgrounds. There is the large industrial concern which wishes the law to be changed to favour its tax position; there is the trade association which wishes a product or a particular way of trading to be removed from actual restriction or the threat thereof; there is the grouping of people who have banded themselves to fight what they see as wrong, such as the armed forces using chemical warfare, or those who wish to improve the opportunities and living conditions of certain categories of disadvantaged persons such as the mentally disturbed.

There are also, as any UK Member of Parliament knows only too well, countless groups of dedicated persons who champion any particular species of animal: half of them want to kill it freely, the other half want to ensure that it leads a golden life and dies of natural causes.

Many such groups of enthusiasts, usually known as pressure groups, carry out their lobbying on their own behalf and devote a great deal of time and effort to doing so. Most businesses and commercial organisations and many well-funded charities and social pressure groups however, employ a professional lobbyist to undertake their campaigns on their behalf. Consequently many public relations companies are now extending their activities to include lobbying which can be seen as a method of helping an organisation relate to its publics, if those publics include legislators and public sector administrators.

A great deal of inaccurate nonsense has been written about lobbying, most of it based upon what people believe goes on in the USA where the profession of lobbyist has long been accepted as being a necessary one but where the person carrying out that function is often assumed to be unethical.

According to Herbert E. Alexander, author of *Money in Politics*: 'In a pluralistic democratic society like that of the United States, it is natural that individuals and groups with abundant economic resources will try to use their wealth to influence the course of government. While money is a common denominator in shaping political power, other ingredients are vital as well: leadership, skill, information, public office, votes, public opinion, legal manoeuvres. . . . Both major parties find supporters in every industry and interest group. . . . The demands of wealth must be tempered to demands that are politically and electorally viable.'

Much of what Mr Alexander says can be applied to the UK but there is no doubt that the outright buying of political influence has gone to far greater lengths in the USA than it ever has in the UK.

In the UK, the lobbyist is a comparatively new phenomenon and is generally saved from temptation towards unethical behaviour by the political and governmental infrastructure which places obtaining accurate information at a higher level than obtaining cash.

Lobbying in the USA is far bigger business than in the UK as a consequence and lobbyists in Washington, of whom there are estimated to be over 9,000 registered and 12,000 unregistered, spend currently some $15 billion annually to achieve their employers' ends: favourable laws or highly profitable contracts.

The situation in Britain is very different. In the USA, individual Congressmen and Senators do appear to be able to make significant amendments to legislation and to influence the award of public sector contracts; individual MPs in the UK can do so rarely. Leaving ethical considerations to one side, it would therefore be pointless to try to exert an improper influence upon them.

The British lobbyist has to be a student of the way that the British system of government works. He has to be aware of which resources it is sensible and ethical to deploy and where to deploy them to the maximum effect so as to influence the vital decision-makers. He must realise that decision-making in the British public sector is a complex process in which parliamentarians and civil servants can both play a significant role; the mix varies according to the circumstances surrounding the decision. The lobbyist must judge the composition of that mix accurately in every case he undertakes.

In order to bring out certain points which must be borne in mind if a lobbying campaign is to be successful, let us follow through a fairly typical day in the life of a lobbyist.

The 'Today' programme on Radio 4 is essential listening for anyone concerned with the warp and woof of British politics. An intelligent and seasoned team are selecting important items for you, commenting on them against a background of informed knowledge and often interviewing the major players involved with healthy scepticism.

Travel time can be used to go through the *Financial Times* and *The Independent*, marking them up for the future filing of stories connected with your client's campaigns. Any time over can be used to scan the serious political journals and trade journals for useful items.

After arriving at the office and making a quick scan of incoming mail for urgent items, the lobbyist then extracts all the relevant items from the previous day's Lords' and Commons' Hansards and other parliamentary papers.

Some of these items may precipitate him into taking immediate action but most will be filed to add to the store of information on how a particular campaign is developing.

In order to be able to judge the relevance of any information that you gather, you must first have ensured that both you and your client are clearly aware of the three basic rules that must be followed in any lobbying campaign.

First, the lobbyist's employer and the lobbyist need to have their aim clearly defined from the start. Second, the achievement of that aim must condition all actions taken. Third, all approaches to parliamentarians and civil servants must be centrally co-ordinated and firm management control must be exercised with the substance of all contacts being put on file promptly.

As the effective day-to-day running of Britain is in the hands of civil servants, the lobbyist should give the civil servant greater priority than politicians. The influence of the average parliamentarian is severely limited and is likely to become more limited still. In the case of most selected industries there will be probably up to 100 parliamentarians who merit the lobbyist's attention outside those holding relevant government posts. If an arbitrary division of time needs to be given as a general guide to the potential lobbyist, it would probably be 65 per cent of available resources to civil servants, 35 per cent to politicians.

What both parliamentarians and civil servants are short of, in varying degrees, is accurate, timely, full information. This is the resource which the lobbyist can deploy to good effect. Well-researched briefing papers are always welcomed. Naturally they will express the point of view of the lobbyist's employing organisation, but this viewpoint must in no way distort the accuracy of the information presented.

Cases must be well argued and must be backed by sound research. If this cannot be done, then the lobbyist has no case to put and that particular campaign cannot be won in the long term.

Because of the division that exists between the cultures of business people and civil servants, one group being profit-orientated, the other service-orientated, the lobbyist acting for industry has to be conscious of the difference in all his approaches to civil servants. In business terms, a 'soft-sell' approach has to be used and any of the characteristics of the hot-shot sales person avoided.

The lobbyist must pace his approach to the less frenetic tempo of the civil service, however much pressure there is for swift action. His first job is to give the civil servants concerned an accurate picture of the organisation he represents, how it works, what its position in the market is and what its particular problems are. He then has to demonstrate how those problems are of legitimate concern to the government, and outline the actions his employers believe should be taken and how these are broadly in line with government policy. Gradually a community of interest must be established, and the civil servants concerned must be supported with a ready supply of factual information and well-prepared briefing material.

When dealing with back-bench MPs. the lobbyist can act at a faster tempo and more positively. Many back-bench MPs feel that their potential is not being fully exploited. They have shown extreme drive and dedication to get to the House of Commons but then find themselves marking time with those very qualities lying dormant. Often, they are looking for a cause or specialisation to make their own, and the lobbyist can act as an information channel to this end. A well-briefed back-bench MP can be very influential both on the floor of the House and in committee.

The lobbyist must also recognise that he is part of a two-way link between those lobbied and his employer. The industrialist/business person has much to learn from the public sector and the lobbyist must function as an effective input channel to his employing organisation.

The lobbyist in the UK needs to strike a balance between the Civil Service and Parliament. The long-term aim should be the creation of a situation wherein a lobbyist's employers are operating in a favourable commercial environment backed by an informed Parliament supporting and guiding the actual implementation of policy by a Civil Service convinced of the rightness of the policy direction being followed.

In order to ensure that the desired level of two-way communication is maintained, the lobbyist holds a monthly meeting with each of his clients, once that particular campaign is well under way. In the early days of a campaign it is probably wiser to meet weekly. These meetings are normally held in the morning to enable him to keep the afternoon clear for parliamentary contacts.

At such a morning meeting he will review progress since the last meeting, raise matters that require immediate attention such as requests for a meeting with a parliamentary committee or a senior civil servant, and plan their actions for the month ahead. The client should be asked to highlight recent major corporate decisions on commercial, personnel and financial policy as any one of these may impact upon a corporate lobbying campaign. Any major up-coming press release should be studied from the viewpoint of its likely impact upon persons in the public sector and permission should be sought for an embargoed early release to parliamentarians or civil servants who are actively concerned with the campaign in question. The lobbyist should review briefly the most recent trends in political thinking that could impact the client's corporate policy and should report on any significant changes in key personnel or power bases. At the end of the meeting both parties should know as much as each other in so far as the progress of the campaign is concerned.

The hours covering the lunch period are too valuable to be allowed to lie fallow. Where possible they should be used to gather in further relevant information or to pass it on to a key target; ideally, it should be possible to do both.

MPs receive a good many invitations to lunch and do not regard them as a great treat. They wish to spend as little time out of the House of Commons as possible and it is wise to arrange for them to be picked up and returned by car. Do not just have them along for a general chat. They will expect to learn something truly useful over the lunch table and are often happy to be asked to do something specific in the cause you are fighting. They may decide to decline but generally they prefer to know exactly what it is you hope to get them to do.

Civil servants do not get many luncheon invitations, not at least until they are fairly senior, and their professional ethics make them inclined to be embarrassed by lavish entertainment. Remember too that the civil servant wishes to become better informed as a result of a meeting with you and will value a factual presentation with as little corporate bias as possible.

After luncheon, the lobbyist will write up the information gathered, highlighting in particular any consequent action needed on his client's part or his own.

For the rest of the afternoon, he will usually be busy in preparing further arguments on behalf of his clients. These may eventually be expressed verbally, as short briefing papers, or as audio/visual presentations. In whatever form they are eventually expressed, it is important that they should be free of any hint of gloss. Neither parliamentarians nor civil servants respond well to glossy, facile presentations with a high picture content. Information should be factual, terse and rather dull in format and layout. The style to aim for is that of a governmental statistical report or of a White Paper. No hint of a commercial presentation should be allowed.

In the early evening he will perhaps pay one of his comparatively rare visits to the House of Commons in order to attend a meeting. There are broadly two schools of thought as to the way that lobbyists should behave in relation to MPs and peers. The old, English school, considers the Houses of Parliament as a club which should, by and large, be left to the club members unless one is invited to visit. The newer, American school of lobbyist regards Westminster as a colony to be exploited by hot-shot salespersons.

This breed of lobbyist spends every possible moment in the Houses of Parliament clutching at the arms of parliamentarians as they pass, whispering in ears and claiming close acquaintance after one short meeting.

Both systems work although the arm-clutching school could produce a reaction against lobbyists on the part of parliamentarians in the long run.

Be that as it may, the lobbyist does attend parliament when he has a job to do that demands his presence there, either to talk to individuals or to attend a meeting of a relevant Select or All Party Committee which is considering a matter of importance to a client. It may be a meeting, held in a Commons Committee Room, of an All Party Committee made up MPs and peers and members of industry, academia and the media; all the members have a particular interest in and knowledge of a particular subject area and the purpose of their meetings is to learn more through presentations from experts followed by a lively debate from the floor. Quite often the minister responsible for the area under debate will come along to make a formal answer to matters raised.

Although the formal part of the meeting is usually informative and useful, it is often the contacts and conversations made before and after the meeting that are of the greatest value to the lobbyist.

The lobbyist will often attend a dinner afterwards in the attractive Harcourt Room of the House of Commons which will be attended by a mixture of senior MPs and peers, industry leaders and experts in the subject under discussion. The contacts made on these occasions and the depth of the discussion advance the knowledge of the lobbyist considerably.

The life of a lobbyist is a full but hardly glamourous one, although he frequently deals with people whose names are well known in places associated with governmental power. Such people and such places are, in fact, dedicated to getting a job done effectively within the framework of a heavy workload. If the lobbyist can help in the achievement of this aim, then he will be welcomed; if not, he will be regarded as a time-wasting nuisance. Information is the currency of exchange and information has to be mined assiduously and continuously.

The life of the lobbyist is largely spent in gathering in information, evaluating it, putting it into a presentable form and then passing it on in the way best suited to the needs of its target audience. The similarity with many other types of public-relations operations is clear. The major difference lies in the nature of the particular public to which the lobbyist is relating. It is a highly specialised one with a particularly high surface visibility but this does not alter the fact that the ultimate aim of the lobbyist is to plan, create and place favourable information about his client within the target public in order to create heightened awareness of his client's organisation so that its business interests may be advanced.

15 Case histories III – VII

Case history III:
Costa del Sol Tourist Board 'UK Tour'

Brief

- To create an immediate impact on the widest possible audience of end-user, ie holiday-maker, by direct contact.

- To raise the profile of Costa del Sol and stimulate demand for the product.

- To gain media exposure in every city visited to further stimulate demand.

Strategy

A Magic Bus Roadshow idea was created for the Costa del Sol Tourist Board's Consumer Roadshow. It visited 23 UK cities during a five-week period.

A five-hour show comprising flamenco dancing, traditional wine-pouring exhibitions, wine sampling, distribution of promotional literature and entry into a holiday prize competition took place at targeted shopping malls, theatres and theme parks throughout the country – and at the Derby.

Results

A 23-city roadshow over a 30-day period, in shopping centres and theme parks up and down the country.

About 143,000 people visited the Bus; trailers for the event and interviews were held with 38 radio stations; 26 photo stories and 14 reports and competitions appeared in the regional press.

CASE HISTORY IV:
RED FOR MEN BY GIORGIO BEVERLY HILLS

Brief

- To introduce Red for Men by Giorgio Beverly Hills, a new, spirited and magnetic fragrance, into the UK market.

- To establish trial by trade and consumer journalists and, most important-ly, the consumer.

- To reinforce and capitalise on the Giorgio Beverly Hills point of difference by creating the image of a Californian, fun and approachable laid-back lifestyle – so different from French fragrance houses.

- To create a synergistic integrated communications approach for Red for Men, through media activity and in-store special events.

Strategy

A creative public relations campaign focused on both trade and consumer media. A unique retailer day was held to enable Giorgio staff and key counter staff to experience the fun and excitement that is Giorgio Beverly Hills.

Trade and consumer press

Red for Men was launched to trade and consumer press at an exclusive cock-tail reception at Mosimann's Restaurant. Samples of Red for Men were given to all trade journalists and interviews with key Giorgio Beverly Hills person-nel were established. One-to-one explanation briefs of Living Flower tech-nology and other essential ingredients of Red for Men were established.

National and regional consumer press were targeted to ensure the inclusion of Red for Men in all fragrance/men's grooming articles. Regular press releases were issued to the press – focusing on fragrance-buying opportuni-ties, ie St Valentine's Day, Father's Day, Christmas.

Additional exciting in-store promotional links were developed, such as the opportunity to win a Red Lotus car by visiting a Giorgio counter and enter-ing a prize draw. Twenty Red Lotus cars were placed in sites nationwide, enhancing in-store animation.

A leading men's magazine linked up with a leading department store to hold a reader event, with opportunity for readers to sample Red for Men and participate in other promotion-related activities.

Retailer event

To build loyalty to Giorgio Beverly Hills and Red for Men, a retailer event was hosted at Millbrook Racetrack and Car Testing Ground, linking with the animated on-going Lotus promotion in stores nationwide. This was the first event of its kind in the UK. Innovative invitations were used to attract the attention of retailers and their families.

To create a taste of fun and excitement, an All-American Cookout was organised with huge barbecue and a multitude of other opportunities for attendees to try, including being driven around the track by Team Lotus, clay pigeon shooting, jumping on a 'flywall' etc.

Results

Red for Men received regular and in-depth coverage in national consumer press; this was matched by consistent and favourable trade press features.

Regional publications specifically focused on special promotions being held in local department stores. The positioning of the Lotus cars at Giorgio Beverly Hills counters increased both traffic in stores and consumer sampling opportunities, and enhanced the image of Giorgio Beverly Hills as a fun and approachable brand.

Red for Men became a key player in the men's fragrance arena.

Red for Men sales were up over 35 per cent above forecast by year end. (Sales of Red fragrance for women increased 19 per cent year on year, due mainly to the successful introduction of Red for Men.)

In retail sales Red for Men entered the top five men's fragrances in the UK.

CASE HISTORY V:
THE JOCKEY Y-FRONT AND JOCKEY FOR HER

Brief

- To launch the restyled Jockey Y-front to the media and consumer.

- To position the Jockey Y-front as the essential undergarment for the modern man and to increase consumer sampling of both brands.

- To increase consumer sampling, build a higher profile and create greater awareness of Jockey for Her.

- To reaffirm Jockey's commitment to quality, comfort and style.

Strategy

Trade

Jockey Y-front: In a creative media-led campaign, regular releases, features and photographs were issued to trade press (both fashion and general marketing publications). Journalists were encouraged to try Jockey garments and to use them in photography. Factory visits by journalists were initiated.

Activity was created on the Jockey stand at trade exhibitions to attract press attention and buyers. Interviews with key Jockey personnel were arranged with the trade press.

Real women: The trade press was informed of unusual promotional activity being used by Jockey for Her USA, eg the use of non-model figure 'Real Women' to appear in promotional material as models.

Consumer

The Jockey and Jockey for Her range were offered to fashion press for use in their photographic shoots. Television stylists were also offered the ranges to use.

Regular entertaining press releases and features examining specific Jockey products were issued to the media, alongside syndicated features detailing underwear trends in general. To increase the trial rate, there were giveaways with leading consumer magazines and regional competitions with targeted regional newspapers.

Real women: National newspapers were encouraged to feature real British women in Jockey for Her.

Jockey Y-front: The Y-front Challenge was issued to selected key fashion writers, asking them to wear Y-fronts for a week instead of their usual undergarments and record their comments. A national photo-call was held to re-launch the Jockey Y-front.

Results

Positive press coverage was achieved for Jockey Y-fronts and Jockey for Her throughout the media. The Y-front Challenge stimulated several underwear features focusing on Jockey Y-fronts throughout the press. A 'library' of quotes from the fashion writers was used in trade and regional releases.

Real Women articles have appeared throughout the consumer press. Jockey for Her has been heralded as a champion of the everyday woman.

Jockey products have been consistently used in fashion and beauty features throughout the press.

Highly successful competitions have appeared in targeted regions.

Jockey personnel are regularly asked to provide commentary on the under-wear market for both television and radio programmes, and have been established as reliable and influential spokespeople.

CASE HISTORY VI:
EMAP GROUP'S CHOICE PUBLICATIONS LIMITED

Brief

- The announcement of a partnership between EMAP's Choice Publications Ltd and French publisher Bayard Presse, and the subsequent relaunch of *Choice* magazine for the over-50s.

- To position Choice Publications as a successful division of the EMAP Group and raise awareness of the 'new' *Choice* magazine among its target audience.

Strategy

A series of face-to-face interviews with the key trade and national business correspondents were set up to discuss details of the partnership.

Key media editors of the national press were lobbied to interview the Editor.

All relevant TV and radio discussion/magazine programmes were contacted. The editor was put forward as an 'expert' pundit on the over-50s – a subject particularly topical at that time.

An independent survey was commissioned to relaunch *Choice* magazine. The survey looked at 'Choices of the '80s' for the over-50s and covered everything from their favourite 'blind date' to the issue which concerned them most. The results were issued to all national and regional media.

The initial launch coverage was followed up on a regular basis with stories related to the more controversial editorial features in *Choice*, eg how safe are our streets and recruiting the over-50s. Material from each issue was also supplied to the Press Association for its monthly syndicated column for the over-50s.

Results

Features in key trade and business press, eg *Campaign*, *Media Week*, *Marketing*, *Magazine Week*, *Newsagent*, *Financial Times*, *Telegraph*, *Independent*.

Interviews with the editor in *The Times*, on BBC Radio 4's 'Woman's Hour' and ITV's 'The Time, The Place' discussion programme.

Launch coverage in the *Daily Star*, *Daily Mirror*, *Sun*, *Daily Mail*, *Daily Express* and more than 70 regional newspapers and radio stations.

Choice magazine attained its position as the national leader in its market and generated considerable interest in the subject of the over-50s.

The magazine exceeded sales targets within three months of the re-launch and, as a result of the coverage in the *Financial Times*, the EMAP share price rose by 6p.

CASE HISTORY VII:
REED EXHIBITIONS 'FAST FOOD FAIR'

Brief

- To reinforce Fast Food Fair's position as the UK's leading annual catering exhibition by extending the range of pre-show editorial coverage in all relevant trade publications.

- To ensure that exhibitors are aware of the publicity opportunities available and encourage them to participate in the PR effort.

- To work with Reed's marketing team to develop at-show promotions.

Strategy

The Publicity Guide which details all publicity opportunities available to exhibitors was revised and developed and key companies were contacted on a regular basis to encourage exhibitor-generated PR.

A number of 'fringe' publications were contacted, in areas such as refrigeration and packaging, with the result that 16 titles now give the show regular coverage.

A comprehensive press pack was issued to all publications in the Publicity Guide, rather than a succession of individual press releases.

At-show promotions were developed to maintain the interest of the press, exhibitors and visitors, including cookery demonstrations, World Food

Workshops and a fitness workout by TV's Lizzie Webb to promote the healthy side of fast food.

An annual news story was created to generate interest from the regional and national consumer media. Stories have included Mexican and Cajun food trends, healthy fast food and food safety.

Results

The fair is now previewed in more than 30 publications and given coverage in a further 70 – an increase of some 300 per cent over the past four years.

Exhibitor awareness of the PR opportunities available has increased by more than 50 per cent with more on-stand promotions and pre-show publicity.

Both press and visitor attendance has risen annually over the past four years and the Fast Food Fair has retained its position as the key event in the catering industry, despite increasing competition from new events.

The size of the exhibition has also increased every year to accommodate the demands of new exhibitors.

Appendix I:
Tourism and the media –
how one industry advises
its members

ENGLISH TOURIST BOARD: *PUBLIC RELATIONS AND THE MEDIA*

The English Tourist Board produces for its members a series of highly readable leaflets on numerous subjects. Its leaflet on PR is particularly popular.

Some of the information contained here has already been covered elsewhere in this book. However, the purpose of this appendix is to illustrate how one industry is tackling its media image and advising its members how to undertake PR.

PUBLIC RELATIONS – *A DEFINITION*

At its simplest, public relations is the business of carefully selecting messages and aiming them effectively at target groups of people. Much of the work of public relations is exploiting channels of communication, of which the most predominant are the press and broadcast media.

However, effective PR can range from employing the right manner in meeting and greeting customers, through to sophisticated sponsorship and even organising campaigns to change the attitude of opinion-formers or legislators – or even the local community.

For example, if you wanted to open up a holiday centre in the vicinity of a quiet seaside town, you might have to employ some skilful PR to convince the local residents of the benefits of such an enterprise. You might try to obtain favourable press coverage locally; or you could call a public meeting to dispel any misgivings and explain the advantages and financial gains to the town from bringing in new business.

PR is always a complementary activity existing alongside other marketing techniques such as advertising, brochure production, direct mail and exhibitions; it can be beneficial to you whatever your line of business – small hotel, self-catering establishment, attraction or conference centre.

HOW DOES PUBLIC RELATIONS DIFFER FROM ADVERTISING?

Many people confuse public relations with advertising – in fact they are quite separate and distinct and their impact on the public is entirely different.

- Advertising is paid for, so you can say what you want (within reason), where you want and as often as you want.

- PR coverage is 'free' but is at the discretion of the media concerned, based on the facts you have presented.

- PR has the advantage of being more credible, since it works through the medium of editorial comment. The media are presumed to be independent and unbiased and their opinions can exert a strong influence on their audience.

INTRODUCING.PUBLIC RELATIONS

Public relations is all about communication and you must determine three key elements before you start.

- What do you want to say? The message is crucial and must be newsworthy if it is to stand a reasonable chance of making any impression, or being taken up by the media.

- Who are you trying to reach? Defining your market is vitally important. Consider your product or service and to whom you think it will appeal most – it's far easier to sell something if you get the market right in the first place.

- What is the best way of reaching your target market? Having decided what your message is and the composition of your target audience, you can then decide which medium to aim for – local or national press, the trade press or local/national radio or TV.

Once these decisions have been made and you have established the size of your budget, you can:

a) engage the services of a professional PR consultancy;

b) employ someone in-house to handle the PR functions;

c) handle some, if not all, of the basic PR functions yourself;

d) use any combination of the above alternatives.

Specific public relations functions

- Initiating media coverage of organisation or company activities, people, services and products through targeted media.

- Writing and issuing press releases to the relevant targeted media, whether trade, local, national or whatever.

- Developing and maintaining contacts with the media and being aware of their needs and interests. It is well worthwhile taking the trouble to get to know the key journalists who cover your sector of the industry. Remember that news reporters are interested in 'hard' news stories that are short and to the point, whereas feature writers are seeking more in-depth material to create longer articles of 1,000 words or more.

- Developing and maintaining a PR information library so that you are ready and prepared when the media calls. This should contain:

  - detailed information describing your business/organisation;

  - short biographical details and photographs of the manager or proprietor and heads of departments;

  - photography to support all releases;

  - specific press releases relating to newsworthy areas of your business;

  - lists of media contacts (press, radio and TV).

- Maintaining a high profile with the local community and others who are in a position to help publicise your product or influence the way in which it is perceived by others.

  - A large number of those who take a holiday in this country stay with friends and relatives and so it is worth the effort to cultivate your local residents so that they can recommend your restaurant, hotel or attraction to their visitors and guests.

  - In every town, city, village or district there are community leaders and those within the business community who are most likely to be of benefit to you. You should be seen as a leader in your own right and in respect of the media you could perhaps have the longer-term aim of becoming the local spokesperson representing your sector of the industry.

CONTACTING THE MEDIA

Dealing with the media in all its forms is one of the most important and most difficult aspects of PR and it is vital that it is handled with professionalism. Many people are wary of journalists, are cagey about giving interviews and often suspicious, if not downright fearful, of them.

Great care has to be given to your choice of spokesperson – ideally a lively and enthusiastic person, not someone who is uncomfortable with the press or feels nervous about being interviewed.

Media lists with named correspondents are regularly published in directories and on floppy discs. Other directories include publication dates, circulation dates and forthcoming supplements (see Further Information). Building your own list is important – and especially in developing lists of specialists and freelance writers.

A word processor, if you have one, will be extremely useful in maintaining lists and editing written material.

PRESS TECHNIQUES

How can you reach and persuade the press to cover your products? Why not start with the telephone – getting your message across quickly to a busy journalist is a refined skill but with practice can be effective.

When calling a journalist, you will probably detect from his or her voice if you have picked a bad moment. Before you plunge into why you have called, ask if it is inconvenient and, if so, arrange a time to call back when the journalist is less likely to be harassed.

However, don't pick up the phone until you have decided what you want to say. Make a list of the points you wish to raise before you dial the number and be prepared for questions and how you will handle any difficult ones. This also applies to areas which you may not wish to discuss!

Equally you can make it easy for the media to contact you or your spokesperson. You may even want to consider giving your home number to a small and selective list of contacts.

MORE FORMAL TECHNIQUES

The press release

This is the main communications tool in public relations but more than 90 per cent of them get filed in the waste bin. Most are far too long and contain too much irrelevant information. The average trade paper can receive around 200 press releases a week, so it is vital to get the structure and content right.

Once you have the idea for a story gather all the pertinent facts. Then ask yourself these important questions: WHO? WHERE? WHAT? WHY? WHEN? HOW?

What an editor needs to know is the answer to these questions. Skill and judgement on your behalf are needed to get them in the right order of importance.

The headline must catch the editor's eye and be suggestive of exciting and interesting information to come, eg the 'who' or 'what' of the story. The opening paragraph should then introduce the story, expanding on the headline and answering more of the above questions.

Succeeding paragraphs should then provide further details in descending order of importance; this enables the editor to shorten the piece from the bottom up when space is limited.

Tell the important part of the story first and always observe the following rules:

- Be specific – never use adjectives or attempt to 'puff' out the story. PR puff is intensely disliked by journalists, so avoid it.

- Avoid the use of jargon, use simple words and sentences.

- Make sure names are spelt correctly.

- Attribute information to a specific person; this gives credibility and reliability to a story.

- The press release should be typed in double-line spacing with wide margins for sub-editors to make changes. Words should never be broken between lines and a paragraph should never be broken between pages.

- If the release is more than one page long, each page should be numbered and clearly indicate that there is more to follow.

- At the end of the release, type in the word 'end' and underneath put a contact for further information, address and telephone number. Also make sure you add the date.

The press conference

This is for major announcements only and affords the opportunity to address several journalists at once. Timing is crucial – obtaining coverage in an evening paper will not be achieved by holding a press conference in the afternoon. Also check that the date does not clash with another press conference or local media event.

Invite the news editors of all the media in your area, selected national media (if appropriate) as well as local dignitaries or officials and other community opinion leaders.

Issue printed invitations. Two days before the event, telephone those who have not replied and compile a list of acceptances.

Prepare a press release detailing the subject of the press conference. Include this in the press kit which should be distributed on arrival.

Ask attendees to sign or print their names in a visitors' book so that you have a record of who attended and also who did not, so that you can arrange for the information to be sent.

Ensure that the press conference briefing is short and to the point.

The press briefing

Face-to-face interviews are among the best means available of obtaining good media coverage and are often more effective than large-scale press gatherings. Journalists prefer exclusive stories and angles, where possible, and are much more likely to play down stories which they know other newspapers have also been given.

If the right reporter from the right paper or magazine (ie in the medium in which coverage of your company would be most advantageous) is invited, excellent results can be achieved.

The press visit or facility trip

This should be planned well in advance and will probably need the collaboration of others, including possibly your regional tourist board. Remember to:

- keep the size of your group to a number that can be easily handled by you;
- make sure the itinerary is an interesting combination of work and pleasure;
- be prepared to be on duty 24 hours a day!

Do not:

- waste journalists' time – don't plan a media visit that lasts five days when it can be accomplished comfortably in three.

Advertorial

Although this will come off your advertising budget, it has become an increasingly important device in achieving coverage. In return for buying advertising space in a certain publication, you will be given editorial coverage free of charge.

Radio and TV

It is not easy to get coverage on national or local television unless something very newsworthy is happening or you create a publicity stunt to bring out the cameras. Local radio, however, presents many more opportunities and it is worth familiarising yourself with all the relevant programmes to see where there may be a chance to exploit your product or service. Producers are often looking for spokespeople.

TIPS FOR DEALING WITH JOURNALISTS

- If a journalist telephones with an enquiry about your property/enterprise or its facilities, ensure that the call is returned as soon as possible. Journalists work to tight deadlines, and failure to respond quickly can result in missed opportunities for media exposure.

- When a journalist is offered facilities, make sure that all the relevant personnel are informed in advance of the visit.

- *Never* tell a journalist anything 'off the record'. If you don't want a journalist to know something, don't tell them.

- When inviting media representatives for meetings, the PRO should do the necessary 'homework' in advance so that everyone is fully briefed on the nature and style of the publication or radio/television programme and knows what angles the journalist is likely to pursue.

- Never ask a journalist who has interviewed you or a member of staff when the article will be published. It places the journalist in an awkward position, and is usually a decision not in the writer's control but in that of the features or news editor.

- Do not over-indulge journalists with food and drink in the belief that this will be an inducement to provide good editorial. Hospitality should be generous, of course, but not 'over the top'.

- Itineraries for journalists should not be too busy. Remember, you want the journalists to experience your product leisurely and comfortably.

- Do not show journalists audio-visuals or videos unless they are professionally produced. Poorly made ones can destroy a carefully built reputation.

- Be very selective about the photo releases you issue to the media. The fact that a 'famous' personality has visited your hotel, restaurant or theme park is no guarantee that the media is likely to be interested in publicising the fact.

- Do not issue photos of groups of people lined up in front of the camera holding drinks. Instead, try to be creative about photo make-up. Creative photos stand a better chance of being used than hackneyed ones.

- Do not mail out press releases to all and sundry and 'hope for the best'. Consider the content of the release and be realistic about which publications are likely to use it. This requires close familiarity with the media and the type of stories and photographs they carry.

PHOTOGRAPHS

Make sure you have a comprehensive library of good, clear black-and-white photographs of your product and of yourself and prominent members of staff. Although colour photos are more attractive and are being increasingly used in glossy magazines, the majority of newspapers and magazines still use black-and-white illustrations extensively.

It is essential that you have access to a reliable local photographer who can be on call at any time. As local newspaper photographers are often willing to undertake freelance work, it may well be worth contacting the picture desk of your local paper.

Caption *all* copies of a photograph as follows:

- Type, double-spaced on the lower half of a sheet of News Release paper, the date, location, the names of people, their positions in the company and any other specific details.

- Lightly glue the four corners of the photograph onto the paper above the caption.

- In the case of a lengthy caption, stick the picture on the reverse of the sheet.

- Identify people by their full names from left to right.

THE MEDIA – ITS STRUCTURE

Editorial coverage of your product in the media is the most tangible result of good PR practice, often producing extra business at low cost. The various media categories you need to consider when drawing up your media lists include the following.

Local

- The daily and evening regional newspapers covering your area as well as weekly newspapers – both those sold and free sheets.
- Local TV and radio stations.
- County magazines and specialist local journals such as regional business magazines.

Local papers should not be underestimated and contacts should be carefully nurtured. Daily and weekly papers are the easiest publications in which to get editorial coverage as there is less competition for space than in the nationals and, by definition, they should be interested in local activities. It is worth familiarising yourself with all the papers – noting their style, type of photographs, the ones which have a travel page or restaurant column, publicise local attractions, etc.

National media

- The 'heavies' – *The Times, Financial Times, The Independent, Guardian, Telegraph*, etc.
- The middle-of-the-roaders – *Daily Mail, Daily Express, Today*, etc.
- The popular press – *Daily Mirror, Sun, Star*, etc.
- National TV and radio.
- Sunday newspapers.

This is a hard nut to crack as there is so much competition for space but it is worth persisting as the rewards are great. A couple of lines about a hotel or attraction can generate a huge amount of interest. The national press will not be interested in parochial matters and you should direct your PR efforts to the feature pages covering travel, hotels, restaurants and attractions relevant to readers from all parts of the country.

Women's and men's interest magazines

Women's interest magazines are very important, particularly as women are often the decision-makers when it comes to holidays or leisure pursuits.

There are more than 40 women's magazines, ranging from the up-market monthly glossies like *Harpers & Queen* to the more homely weeklies like *My Weekly*. Not all carry pages which would be appropriate, but many have travel pages or carry other relevant sections. Do note, however, that monthly magazines usually have a copy deadline of at least three months before publication, so it is essential to plan well in advance. There are also an increasing number of magazines specifically for men, for example *GQ*, *Arena* and *Esquire*.

Specialist magazines

These include sporting magazines, business publications and many other categories that may be applicable to your operation.

If you have a nine-hole golf course, include the golfing journals in news of special golf weekends; if some rare species has been sighted near your hotel, let the ornithology journals know of your existence.

Trade press

- Travel trade press.
- Catering press.
- Conference press.

The trade press needs rather different treatment from the consumer press but it is well worth putting in the effort to get coverage in the 'bibles' of the travel and hotel industry. They are essentially papers which report and reflect all the changes and developments in a changing industry. Use them not only to keep abreast of what is going on in tourism and travel but try to develop news items or statements for publication.

CRISIS PUBLIC RELATIONS

An equally important, but not always fully appreciated, aspect of good PR work involves handling 'bad news'. Just as good news can increase your business, so bad publicity can damage or even ruin it. Should bad publicity strike, you must be equipped to deal with it. While prevention is always better than cure, realistically it is not always possible to prevent something happening which may damage your image, but at least you can be prepared.

First, isolate the possible 'disasters' which could befall your business, eg food poisoning, fires, deaths, accidents, etc.

Second, draw up a plan in advance of how you would handle the media in any given crisis situation.

- Agree on the spokesperson – all enquiries should be channelled through the spokesperson in order that replies are consistent.

- Prepare and warn other staff about talking to the media.

- Make sure you have on file the home telephone numbers of management so that you can contact them out of office hours.

And if the worst should happen:

- Prepare draft statements that clarify your company's position.

- If you don't have all the facts, keep calm and explain that you will provide more details as you have them to hand. In most circumstances an initial stagement such as 'we are investigating the incident' will suffice until a more detailed response has been researched and prepared.

Hopefully a major crisis, such as loss of life, will not arise in your career. If it should, remember that the press also have a job to do and if you will not help them to get the facts, they will obtain them from elsewhere or use conjecture. It is better to be honest and if you don't know all the details, say so, and then say when you expect to have them.

NON-PRESS TECHNIQUES

Although the main component of PR is dealing with the media, there are other ways of getting the message across to your target audiences:

- By creating and maintaining links with others involved in tourism, such as the regional tourist board, the tourist information centres, local handling agents, coach companies and car hire firms. Through these you may be able to participate in joint promotions or receive extra business through word-of-mouth.

- By holding 'open days' for the press and/or local residents.

- By attending exhibitions and travel workshops, which provide a ready marketplace for you to meet the press, tour operators, travel agents and (sometimes) members of the public.

- By speaking at trade seminars and conferences, thus raising the profile of your business/organisation within the business community.

- Through personal PR; always being courteous, remembering past visitors and their families and interests, perhaps sending a Christmas card to former customers.

FURTHER INFORMATION

Ask whether your local library has the following publications:

THE INSTITUTE OF PUBLIC RELATIONS
The Old Trading House, 15 Northburgh Street, London EC1V 0PK. Tel: 071-253 5151

Can provide details of courses in public relations and information on text-books.

CHARTERED INSTITUTE OF MARKETING
Moor Hall, Cookham, Maidenhead, Berkshire SL6 9QH. Tel: 062-85 24922

Short residential courses.

WILLINGS PRESS GUIDE
Reed Information Services, Windsor Court, East Grinstead House, East Grinstead, West Sussex TH19 1XA. Tel: 0342 326972

Annual publication, containing details of publications and periodicals in the UK and overseas (publication dates, contacts, circulation figures, etc.)

HELP FROM THE TOURIST BOARDS

You may find that you require specialist help in organising your PR campaign.

Each regional tourist board provides a range of services for commercial members which include familiarisation visits by press, mailings, photographic libraries and joint promotions.

The regional tourist board will also be able to tell you about any possibilities of gaining press coverage through the English Tourist Board and the British Tourist Authority, and advise you if they feel you could benefit from seeking assistance from a professional PR consultancy.

English Tourist Board Marketing Advice Sheets published to date:

'Effective Media Advertising'

'Effective Design and Print'

'Direct Mail – A Step by Step Introduction'

'Public Relations and the Media'

'Researching Your Market'

'Marketing a Visitor Attraction'

'Marketing a Small Guest House or Bed & Breakfast'

'Profiting from Exhibitions'

'Maximising Your Conference Potential'

If you have any queries or want more copies of this or other Marketing Advice Sheets, please contact Marketing Advisory Services, English Tourist Board, Thames Tower, Black's Road, Hammersmith, London W6 9EL, Tel: 081-563 3361/3364.

Appendix II: Public relations photography techniques

Alastair McDavid, Director, Thistle Photography, London

Without a good photograph the press won't give much space to even the best of stories. Most PR people claim to know this but few do much about it, perceiving that the press release is much more important than creating a photo opportunity.

Readers immediately notice a good photograph, but unless something catches their eye, they may miss a good story.

WHAT ARE YOU UP AGAINST?

The editor of a weekly trade publication has said he receives on average 800 press releases a week, of which about 200 are accompanied by photographs: of those 200 photographs, 80 per cent are rejected for poor technical quality and/or boring content, leaving just 40 photographs competing for space in the publication.

He went on to say, 'We control the printed word: we can shorten it, or – via a phone call to the person who sent it – lengthen it. In fact we can re-vamp it to suit our style and still meet our deadline. With the accompanying photograph we're stuck with it. We can crop it or drop it.'

He continued, 'If a story is a little weak, we will sometimes use it as a filler. However, a good photograph, even accompanying a weak story, can still be used as a captioned pic on its own merit. We take pride in the appearance of our paper, so we will position the photograph to give visual impact.'

So an item that may have merited just three square inches somewhere in the paper is transformed into 30 square inches in an eye-catching position. Four times as many people read photo captions as body copy and it is said that the average picture in a trade paper/journal takes up space that would cost you at least £300 to buy; it is also a generally recognised fact that editorial is worth six times more than advertising in getting your message over. So fudging the next photo session could cost you at least £1,800.

ANALYSE YOUR COMPETITION

Every publication is different but, as a guide to find out what picture editors select, it is well worth taking the trouble to thumb through back issues of those publications to which you regularly submit press releases and analyse why the editor selected the photographs used. If necessary, mark each photograph out of ten so that you can really study it – content, news value, message, fun, background, technical quality (ie, is it in focus?). Get a feel for the sort of photos they run with and if any type of photograph is used again and again, it could work for you; how could you improve on the shot? With colour photographs, what colours feature strongly: yellow and red? Was the colour introduced into the photograph by use of props?

Count up the number of head-and-shoulder shots compared to other submitted photographs; it generally works out about 30–40 per cent but in many publications the figure is higher. It is therefore vital to have a set of up-to-date, stock, head-and-shoulder photographs of key personnel, taken against a plain white background (a projection screen is perfect) without shadows.

FILM TYPES AND THEIR USES

You will need to know the three basic types of film a photographer will use. It is worth mentioning, without going into the technical details, that manufacturers produce many variations of each film type – versions for low light, interior lighting, etc – therefore photographers depend on your brief to ensure that they bring the right version of the films to the job. You will be more concerned with selecting the right film for ultimate use for which the photographs are intended.

Black-and-white film: when processed, the film used in the camera produces a black and white (b/w) negative. The negative is then printed – a second process – to produce b/w prints on photographic paper.

This is the natural choice for most PR shots going to newspapers or journals reproducing in b/w and it is cheap.

Colour negative film: when processed, the film used in the camera produces a colour negative. The negative is then printed – a second process – to produce colour prints on photographic paper.

Use this film, when all, or the majority, of your needs are for colour prints: national newspapers using colour, to insert into an album of the event, to give guests a photograph, to use as sales aids for your product rather than have a brochure printed, etc.

Black-and-white prints as well as colour transparencies can be made from colour negative film.

Colour transparency film: when processed, the film used in the camera is *now* a colour transparency. You will be given the film that *went through the camera*. They are *original transparencies*. Hold them up to the light and you can see a colour photograph.

Do not lose or damage them: unlike b/w and colour negative film where you can just phone up the photographer and order another print, with colour transparency film *there are no negatives*. Use a courier or registered post to forward irreplaceable transparencies.

A b/w or colour print can be produced from a colour transparency by your photographer producing the appropriate negative from your original transparency. You can also make a duplicate transparency from the original transparency.

Colour transparencies are often referred to as 'slides' when the 35mm size of film is used: they are an obvious choice for an audio-visual (AV) presentation. Remember that most slick AV presentations require horizontal rather than upright shots.

For colour reproduction in magazines the printing process requires colour transparencies in the majority of cases. However, with the introduction of new printing technology, it is worth checking this, as many weekly trade journals and most national papers now use colour prints instead.

WHAT SORT OF PHOTOGRAPH WILL EDITORS USE?

- Ask them.
- News value and exclusivity will appeal to any editor.
- Check back-issues.
- Keep groups small: two or three, four at most, if they have to be named.

- People: come in close; faces matter, even if the background is important.

- An action photograph, with props or product. People doing something.

- Avoid cluttered backgrounds.

- Fill the whole picture area; draw a sketch beforehand if necessary.

- Colour: strong colours (reds and yellows stand out).

- Fun or 'unusual poses' shots.

- Crisp, sharp – professional – photographs.

- Good head-and-shoulders, shadowless white background.

- Pictures that arrive on time!

PLANNING THE PHOTO SESSION

It is essential to plan for that 'first' photograph. The PRO needs to ensure that the concept and contents meet their company's/client's media requirements. Get it in the bag right at the start; then, no matter what happens, you are covered. As the session progresses you can move on to variations which evolve on the day. If you have a separate PR requirement in addition to a photo-call, do this well in advance of the press turning up. It will also give you time to ensure that you provide invited photographers with the idea you're trying to get across. They will then tell you what they want!

Do not confuse a photo-call with a press-call: journalists may be happy to sit through a press briefing, but press photographers won't – they will want to be invited at a time when they have instant access to the subjects to be photographed, so they can 'do the job' and quickly move on to the next assignment.

The following eleven points will help you plan the session:

What am I going to do with the photographs? This is really the most vital question of all and, should someone else ask you to book a photographer, find out what they are going to do with the photographs.

What do I want them to achieve? Just a reminder/record of the event or set-up? Internal or external PR? Requirement to illustrate a product or a person? What company image is required? Is there an obvious message? Will it come across in the photograph or in the press release or do I have to create a photo opportunity?

Who is going to receive the photographs? This will decide the type of film used, the style of photograph for the publication(s) involved and whether different shots are required to offer exclusive photos to competing media. For exclusive shots, make them *totally* different, not just a change of personnel. If it's a colour publication, introduce colour.

Publication deadlines? First, this allows you to inform the photographer of your required turnround time and to plan the timing and date of the event to ensure that 'hot' news stories reach editors' desks in time for the next edition. News and sports pages apart, most daily papers 'close off' pages at about 2.00 pm, the very pages that a good PR photo and story stand a chance of getting into. Second, you may need to prepare caption and address labels in advance so that the photos can go direct from the photographers.

How many people are involved? Are they under my control? People like to be told in advance that they are required for a photograph. Tell them. Bring them under your control, give them a precise time, location, etc and your requirements of them by producing a shooting list. Some celebrities may not allow flash photography because it irritates their eyes, particularly sports personalities who have agreed to 'pop' into your marquee between events to meet your guests.

People also turn up late or fail to turn up at all, not realising that it wasn't a 'free' lunch but their presence in a photo which was the cornerstone of your whole PR campaign.

Many photographs are taken at conferences. Often it will be necessary to pose some photographs on the set before the conference starts, during a break or right at the end, for a whole host of reasons. Inform the producer that you will need both the time and his assistance to have spotlights dimmed and the correct slide up on the back projection unit, etc. If you decide to take the shots during rehearsal, remind everyone not to arrive in casual clothes.

If you decide to use professional models for a session, they will ask you what clothes you require them to bring and the image you wish them to project. If you use your own staff, run through the same procedure and vet their clothes if necessary! If you are depending on Joe Public – 'we'll just grab someone off the street' – be ready for a long wait. They don't look like 'normal' people and never fit the image you visualised. The use of friends, colleagues or models is usually more cost-effective and produces better results.

Location of shoot? Interior or exterior? If exterior, check time of day and position of sun – particularly important when you cannot move buildings around to get the name of the company in the background. Remember that during the winter months photographic daylight is poor for some action/exterior shots. It gets dark at 3.30 pm. Before shooting, check whether you need permission or a permit.

Look carefully at your backgrounds. This is particularly important if you have to do a shoot requiring various locations in an office or factory. Organise any 'maintenance' in advance – poor paintwork, rubbish clearing, damaged product in a warehouse. Broken venetian blinds and burnt-out lightbulbs are a classic time-waster on a shoot. It is useful if you are using an unfamiliar venue to ensure that a maintenance person is on hand, often just to locate the light switches or a ladder. A polaroid camera is a useful way of checking out a location in advance: defects will stand out. Parked vehicles with unlocatable drivers are another irritation.

Props: Props can be either a logo, the product or introduced items such as a bottle of champagne, hats, costumes or giant scissors to cut the ribbon – a wide colourful ribbon, not a thin tape etc. In all cases it also gives the subjects of the photograph something to do and turns it into a 'doing' photograph. It is often better to emphasis the prop by making it larger than life size.

You should have a set of stock 'company props'. The range should cover the company logo in various sizes, plus a 35mm transparency, an overhead projection slide or a disk if computers are used: large photographs of your product(s), name plates for key personnel, flags, hard hats with company name on etc. Using number plates with the company name, or initials to stick over existing ones, can avoid dating photographs by the registration letter.

When do I need the results? Remember to notify the photographer in advance. They may need to organise their lab to be standing by and to arrange for a messenger bike to rush the films back. Again, if you need urgent prints, advise on a rough quantity in advance.

Can it be a stand-alone photograph? A classic example of this type of photograph is a pools winner with a giant cheque. The name of the pools company, the amount won and the winner are clearly identified.

Is the picture stronger than the story? If so, you can even write a press release to complement the photo. This often results when a bonus unplanned photograph just 'happens' on a shoot.

Pre-sell a photo? Have a chat to the journalist/editor to see what their thoughts are about the story, find out what type of photo they would run with – do they want an exclusive?

Booking and briefing a photographer: If you are lucky enough to have time on your side, you should just book the photographer's time until you formulate your plans for the event. The key details are date, time, duration, venue and job title.

BRIEFING A PHOTOGRAPHER

- In the age of fax, it's very simple to confirm bookings and requirements on a pre-printed order form to suit your business, which ensures that all the salient points are covered. A sample is shown below:

PR PHOTOGRAPHY SESSION ORDER

From: _____ Date: _____ PO no: _____

Photo session title: _____

Date: _____ Start time: _____ Duration: _____

Client: _____

Location address: _____

_____

Location contact: _____ & phone number: _____

Required: B/W Δ Colour negative Δ Transparency $2\frac{1}{2}$ Δ 35mm Δ AV use Δ

Indoor Δ Outdoor Δ Head/shoulders Δ Group photo Δ Of: ____ people
TV/Other photographers present Δ General press photocall Δ

Brief: _____

_____

_____

_____

End result: Trade press Δ National Δ In-house Δ General Δ

Contacts/transparencies required: Date: _____ Time: _____

Rush print order to follow: Approximately _____ prints

Checklist: Map / Invitation / Permit / Logos / Props / Book room for head/shoulders
Dress: Black tie, lounge suits, jeans & wellies / Model release form / Pass

It is vital for the person who is assuming control of the shoot to brief the photographer personally, so that not only can ideas be bounced around between you but also both parties can ask questions and get a feel for the job and schedule. If you can fax a programme or details through first, do so. Run through the following:

- Give every job a 'job title' which will appear in your records, the photographer's files and on the invoice.

- Brief outline: reason for photographs, who will receive them. If it's a particular target publication unfamiliar to the photographer, send them a copy so they can see the style.

- Location, contact and location telephone number.

- Time you want shooting to start (if you say 10.45 am for 11.00 am start, it avoids any confusion) and duration.

- Appropriate film type: colour, b/w, transparency. If it's transparency, do you want 35mm slides for an AV?

- Number of people involved: necessary for giving scale to a job and ensuring enough film is available and the lighting equipment is correct for a large group shot.

- Is TV/video involved? Both could hinder the photographer's movements and they may want to bring additional equipment.

- Is it a general photo-call? Again, an equipment choice.

- Deadline for contacts or transparency film.

- Approximate quantity of prints, and deadline if urgent.

- Is flash photography allowed?

- Attire for photographer.

- Now check that you've added your photographer to the guest list so all information sent to guests/journalists is also forwarded, along with any invitations, directions, passes etc, to the photographer.

PRACTICAL POINTS

If the shoot involves lots of people or a large number of shots, it is a good idea to have a shooting list: hand it to those involved so that they realise you have a specific PR requirement for a certain number of photographs and try to do the shots one after another. For some reason executives and guests of honour get annoyed if you keep dragging them back for yet another photo if they have got a drink in their hand and are mingling. Shooting lists also serve as an effective way of gently telling people they are *not* required in a photograph.

Think of ways of introducing colour to make your picture stand out and get used. Ask men to wear a bright tie, to contrast against dark suits; ask women to dress in bright colours rather than black.

Use coloured name badges to identify particular types of guests, especially if you do not know them and need to have shots showing a mix of guests. This applies, for example, when each member of a trade association invites the local MP to an annual lunch and your requirement is to get photographs of MPs talking to association members with only half an hour during the pre-lunch drinks to get the shots. It always happens that you are called away or busy and you need the photographer to operate on their own. It is vital to identify journalists, as no publication is going to use a photograph containing a journalist from a rival publication; nor do they usually publish 'staff' in their own publication.

It is a lot quicker and easier to use a micro-recorder to take down names and titles rather than do it by long hand. If it is a large function, do not ask the photographer to take down the names but allow them to concentrate on photography. Supply a member of your own staff, who is familiar with the guest list and your own personnel.

Safety at events such as factory/plant openings, open days, etc is particularly important when you have other photographers present who are not under your control. Make sure that everyone understands the safety rules by having both your own staff briefing and one for invited guests/press. Then be on constant guard for obvious errors, particularly in the background: no hard hats, no eye protection, people under cranes/hoists, etc.

If you commission a photographer, you have control over the shoot and the distribution of the results. You are able to withhold poor, unflattering photographs. With the press, you have no control over their results, either those used immediately to publicise the event or those used some time in the future when the negatives are pulled from the files and a different shot is used.

Do allow enough time for a photographic session and advise your subjects accordingly. Nothing is more counterproductive than when, after two shots of the chairman handing over the cheque, he starts apologising to the recipient about having to have the photos taken, particularly if you need b/w for the press, colour transparencies for your house magazine and colour prints for the recipient . . . it all takes time.

An 8" × 6" b/w print is the most cost-effective size, large enough for the editor to 'get the picture' and plan his cropping if necessary. The additional cost of a 10" × 8" b/w, the larger envelope and higher postage can add more than 30 per cent to the bill.

A 35mm slide is obviously more cost effective for AV presentations; for colour reproduction in magazines, a $2\frac{1}{4}$" square (medium format) transparency is preferred.

The majority of PR photography involves manipulating people. Once the photographic session is under way, your photographer must, without exception, have the ability to motivate everybody in the view-finder. If they do not have an instant rapport with the subjects, you are using the wrong photographer for the job.

CAPTIONING PRINTS/TRANSPARENCIES

Picture editors' desks are covered in photos, captions and press releases; the last thing you want is for a good photo to become separated from its caption.

Sometimes editors are too busy to match up separated prints from their photo captions on bits of paper – so they bin them.

At the end of the day they put some pictures on hold for tomorrow and send others off to the picture library . . . but only if they are captioned:

If it's exclusive, say so. It had better be exclusive, as picture editors have long memories. They even have a list!

If you are successful, the press release goes to a journalist, and the photo and caption go down to production. Now you can see why it's so important to ensure that the caption sticks with the photograph. With Nationals and dailies, if you send a photo and press release to, say, the consumer editor, send the same photo and caption to the picture editor.

Don't expect them to be returned to you, no matter what is promised.

PRINTS

- No paper clips.
- No staples.
- No sellotape.
- No writing on the back of prints.

Use adhesive labels, preferably pre-printed with the name of your company, address, phone number, and then include the following typed on the label:

- Date.

- Story/photo title – to match your press release.

- Captions, from left to right. Full names (John Smith, not J. Smith).

- Contact name at your company.

Affix this to the back of the print.

TRANSPARENCIES

Type the following onto your letterhead:

- Date.

- Story/photo title – to match your press release.

- Captions, from left to right. Full names (John Smith, not J. Smith).

- Contact name at your company.

Using a glue stick or double-sided tape, stick a transparency bag onto the letterhead and slip the transparency inside. The editor can then slip the transparency out, view it and safely return it to keep with the caption.

POINTS TO REMEMBER ABOUT SUBMITTING PHOTOGRAPHS

- Many publications are using colour prints nowadays – check.

- If you have an upright and a landscape of the same shot, it's a good idea to send both – it doubles your chance to fit the space shape they may have available.

- If it's an original transparency, don't expect it to be returned, even if you ask.

- If it's a valuable transparency, make a duplicate. Decide whether you are going to keep the duplicate or original yourself. Some magazines will only accept originals – check.

- Always send original transparencies by courier or registered post if it's irreplaceable or guaranteed use.

- If there is something on a transparency that must not be printed in a publication (say, a person or logo, which you can crop out), then use scissors to cut the transparency – don't rely on a request on the photo caption or a pen mark on the bag.

- You can crop a transparency when you duplicate – often at no extra cost if you use the right photographers!

- Just send the best transparency: don't send a strip of the shoot, where some are obviously bad, eg one person with eyes closed or looking away. Don't risk the wrong one being used.

- If you have arranged with a trade paper an exclusive page or spread of pictures, say, an awards ceremony or promotional evening, it's usual to send the editor every transparency taken in their acetate sleeves. Go through the transparencies, chinagraph around the best transparency in each caption heading and number it to match your caption sheet.

PLACING PRINT/DUPLICATING ORDERS

Placing print orders, duplicate transparencies and copy negatives can all result in delay and costly expense (on both sides) if not done correctly.

A transparency sent through the post with 'two prints of this please' written on a scrap of paper is not helpful! Common problems are lack of deadline date, no print size indicated and no job title or identifier on material sent in for duplicating or copying which eventually causes you problems when the invoice just states 'person at desk'.

From the lab's point of view, PRO's often identify film wrongly, for example by saying that they are couriering over a colour negative for rush print when in fact it's a colour transparency. So the quoted price and production time, leading to delivery time, are all wrong.

In some cases you'll be ordering from negatives held by your photographer, in others you'll be forwarding negatives, artwork (prints) or transparencies to your photographer.

To avoid confusion you should have a master form to ensure that you always address the basic points with every order – see list below:

Contact name:
Date of order:
Purchase order number:
Job title or photographer's job number:
Number of transparencies/prints/artwork enclosed:
Deadline date:
Rush required (costs extra):

Price required before proceeding: Yes/No
Prints will be put into our own folders/frames (check size):

Results required:
- Colour print, b/w print or transparency
- Size
- Quantity
- Crop as per instructions
- In/not in folders
- In/not in mounts: plastic/glass/card

Remember to state whether you want 35mm dupe transparencies from medium-format transparencies cropped horizontally for AV slides.

THE RESULT

When you commission a photographer, the charge is exactly the same for a photograph that gets splashed across the front page as for one that ends up on the editor's spike!

Appendix III:
The top media

DAILY EXPRESS
Ludgate House, 245 Blackfriars Road, London SE1 9UX
Tel: 071-928 8000, Fax: 071-620 1654

DAILY MAIL
Northcliffe House, 2 Derry Street, London W8 5TT
Tel: 071-938 6000, Fax: 071 937 4463

DAILY MIRROR
Holborn Circus, London EC1P 1DQ
Tel: 071-353 0246, Fax: 071-822 3405

DAILY SPORT
19 Great Anscoats Street, Manchester M60 4BT
Tel: 061- 236 4466, Fax: 061-236 4535

DAILY STAR
Ludgate House, 245 Blackfriars Road, London SE1 9UX
Tel: 071-928 8000, Fax: 071 922 7960

THE DAILY TELEGRAPH
1 Canada Square, Canary Wharf, London E14 5DT
Tel: 071-538 5000, Fax: 071-538 6242

EVENING STANDARD
Northcliffe House, 2 Derry Street, London W8 5EE
Tel: 071-938 6000, Fax: 071 937 3193

FINANCIAL TIMES
1 Southwark Bridge, London SE1 9HL
Tel: 071-873 3000, Fax: 071-873 3076

THE GUARDIAN
119 Farringdon Road, London EC1R 3ER
Tel: 071-278 2332, Fax: 071-837 2114

THE INDEPENDENT
40 City Road, London EC1Y 2DB
Tel: 071-253 1222, Fax: 071 956 1435

MORNING STAR
1–3 Ardleigh Road, London N1 4HS
Tel: 071-254 0033, Fax: 071-254 5950

THE SUN
1 Virginia Street, London E1 9XP
Tel: 071-782 4000, Fax: 071-488 3253

THE TIMES
1 Pennington Street, London E1 9XN
Tel: 071-782 5000, Fax: 071-488 3242

TODAY
1 Virginia Street, Wapping, London E1 9BS
Tel: 071-782 4600, Fax: 071-782 4822

NATIONAL SUNDAY NEWSPAPERS

THE INDEPENDENT ON SUNDAY
40 City Road, London EC1Y 2DB
Tel: 071-253 1222, Fax: 071-956 1469

THE MAIL ON SUNDAY
Northcliffe House, 2 Derry Street, London W8 5TS
Tel: 071-938 6000, Fax: 071-937 3829

NEWS OF THE WORLD
1 Virginia Street, London E1 9XR
Tel: 071-782 4000, Fax: 071-583 9504

THE OBSERVER
Chelsea Bridge House, Queenstown Road, London SW8 4NN
Tel: 071-627 0700, Fax: 071-627 5570

THE PEOPLE
Holborn Circus, London EC1P 1DQ
Tel: 071-353 0246, Fax: 071-822 3864

SUNDAY EXPRESS
Ludgate House, 245 Blackfriars Road, London SE1 9UX
Tel: 071-928 8000, Fax: 071-922 7964

SUNDAY MIRROR
Holborn Circus, London EC1P 1DQ
Tel: 071-353 0246, Fax: 071-822 2160

SUNDAY SPORT
3rd Floor, Marten House, 39–47 East Road, London N1 6AH
Tel: 071-251 2544, Fax: 071-608 1979

SUNDAY TELEGRAPH
1 Canada Square, Canary Wharf, London E14 5DT
Tel: 071-538 5000, Fax: 071-513 2504

THE SUNDAY TIMES
1 Pennington Street, London E1 9XW
Tel: 071-782 5000, Fax: 071-782 5658

NATIONAL DAILY COLOUR SUPPLEMENTS

ES – EVENING STANDARD MAGAZINE
Northcliffe House, 2 Derry Street, London W8 5EE
Tel: 071-938 6000, Fax: 071-937 9302

THE INDEPENDENT MAGAZINE
40 City Road, London EC1Y 2DB
Tel: 071-253 1222, Fax: 071-962 0016

THE TELEGRAPH MAGAZINE
1 Canada Square, Canary Wharf, London E14 5DT
Tel: 071-538 5000, Fax: 071-513 2504

NATIONAL SUNDAY COLOUR SUPPLEMENTS

OBSERVER MAGAZINE
Chelsea Bridge House, Queenstown Road, London SW8 4NN
Tel: 071-627 0700, Fax: 071-627 5572

PEOPLE MAGAZINE
Daily Mirror Building, 33 Holborn Circus, London EC1P 1DQ
Tel: 071-822 3121, Fax: 071-822 3405

SUNDAY EXPRESS MAGAZINE
Ludgate House, 245 Blackfriars Road, London SE1 9UX
Tel: 071-928 8000, Fax: 071-928 7262

SUNDAY MAGAZINE
5th Floor, Phase 2, 1 Virginia Street, Wapping, London E1 9BD
Tel: 071-782 7194, Fax: 071-782 7474

SUNDAY MIRROR MAGAZINE
3rd Floor, Orbit House, Holborn Circus, London EC1P 1DQ
Tel: 071-353 0246, Fax: 071-583 4151

SUNDAY TIMES MAGAZINE
1 Pennington Street, London E1 9XW
Tel: 071-782 7000, Fax: 071-867 0410

TELEGRAPH MAGAZINE
1 Canada Square, Canary Wharf, London E14 5DT
Tel: 071-538 5000, Fax: 071-513 2500

YOU – MAIL ON SUNDAY MAGAZINE
Northcliffe House, 2 Derry Street, London W8 5TS
Tel: 071-938 6000, Fax: 071-938 1488

NATIONAL TELEVISION

BBC BREAKFAST NEWS
BBC Television Centre, Wood Lane, London W12 7RJ
Tel: 081-576 7506, Fax: 081-749 7872

BBC TELEVISION DOCUMENTARIES
Room 1065, Kensington House, Richmond Way, London W14 0AX
Tel: 081-895 6322, Fax: 081-749 8378

BBC TELEVISION NEWS
Room 6234 Spur, Television Centre, Wood Lane, London W12 7RJ
Tel: 081-743 8000 x 1914, Fax: 081-749 6972

BBC TELEVISION NEWS & CURRENT AFFAIRS
BBC White City, 201 Wood Lane, London W12 7TS
Tel: 081-752 5252, Fax: 081-752 7009

BBC WORLD SERVICE TELEVISION
BBC Television Centre, Wood Lane, London W12 7KJ
Tel: 081-576 1972, Fax: 081-749 7435

CHANNEL 4 NEWS
200 Grays Inn Road, London WC1X 8XZ
Tel: 071-833 3000, Fax: 071-430 4608

CHANNEL 4 TELEVISION
60 Charlotte Street, London W1P 2AX
Tel: 071-631 4444, Fax: 071-580 2618

GMTV
The London Television Centre, Upper Ground, London SE1 9TT
Tel: 071-827 7000, Fax: 071-827 7249

INDEPENDENT TELEVISION NEWS
200 Gray's Inn Road, London WC1X 8XZ
Tel: 071-833 3000, Fax: 071-430 4019

NATIONAL RADIO

BBC EVENTS UNIT
BBC World Service, Information Centre, LG35 Centre Block, Bush House,
London WC2B 4PH
Tel: 071-257 2189, Fax: 071-497 8156

BBC RADIO 1
Broadcasting House, London W1A 1AA
Tel: 071-580 4468

BBC RADIO 2
Broadcasting House, London W1A 1AA
Tel: 071-580 4468

BBC RADIO 3
Broadcasting House, London W1A 1AA
Tel: 071-580 4468

BBC RADIO 4
Broadcasting House, London W1A 1AA
Tel: 071-580 4468

BBC RADIO 5
Broadcasting House, London W1A 1AA
Tel: 071-927 5552, Fax: 071-580 0187

BBC RADIO NEWS & CURRENT AFFAIRS
Room 3105, Broadcasting House, London W1A 1AA
Tel: 071-580 4468, Fax: 071-636 4295

BBC WORLD SERVICE
Export Liaison, PO Box 76, Bush House, Strand, London WC2B 4PH
Tel: 071-240 3456, Fax: 071-240 4635

CLASSIC FM
Academic House, 24–28 Oval Road, London NW1 7DQ
Tel: 071-284 3000, Fax: 071-284 2835

INDEPENDENT RADIO NEWS (IRN)
200 Grays Inn Road, London WC1X 8X2
Tel: 071-430 4814, Fax: 071-430 4834

GLOSSY MAGAZINES

COUNTRY HOMES & INTERIORS
King's Reach Tower, Stamford Street, London SE1 9LS
Tel: 071-261 6433, Fax: 071-261 6895

COUNTRY LIVING
National Magazine House, 72 Broadwick Street, London W1V 2BP
Tel: 071-439 5000, Fax: 071-439 5093

ELLE
Rex House, 4–12 Lower Regent Street, London SW1Y 4PE
Tel: 071-930 9050, Fax: 071-839 2762

HARPERS & QUEEN
National Magazine House, 72 Broadwick Street, London W1V 2BP
Tel: 071-439 5000, Fax: 071-439 5506

HOMES & GARDENS
King's Reach Tower, Stamford Street, London SE1 9LS
Tel: 071-261 5000, Fax: 071-261 6247

HOUSE & GARDEN
Vogue House, Hanover Square, London W1R 0AD
Tel: 071-499 9080, Fax: 071-493 1345

MARIE CLAIRE
Mercury House, 195 Knightsbridge, London SW7 1RE
Tel: 071-261 5240, Fax: 071-261 5277

SHE
National Magazine House, 72 Broadwick Street, London W1V 2BP
Tel: 071-439 5000, Fax: 071-439 5350

VOGUE
Vogue House, Hanover Square, London W1R 0AD
Tel: 071-499 9080, Fax: 071-493 1345

NATIONAL NEWS AGENCIES

ASSOCIATED PRESS NEWS AGENCY
12 Norwich Street, London EC4A 1BP
Tel: 071-353 1515, Fax: 071-353 8118

NATIONAL NEWS AGENCY
30 St John's Lane, London EC1M 4BJ
Tel: 071-490 7700, Fax: 071-250 1204

PRESS ASSOCIATION
85 Fleet Street, London EC4P 4BE
Tel: 071-353 7440, Fax: 071-936 2363

REUTERS LTD
85 Fleet Street, London EC4P 4AJ
Tel: 071-250 1122, Fax: 071-583 3769

UNITED PRESS INTERNATIONAL
2 Greenwich View Place, Millharbour, London E14 9NN
Tel: 071-538 5310, Fax: 071-538 1051

LOCAL RADIO STATIONS

Most local radio stations offer a music-based service with local news, weather and traffic bulletins. A few offer a more substantial news/information service, including the following:

RADIO BORDERS
(The Borders)
Tel: (0896) 59444

CITY FM
(Merseyside)
Tel: 051-227 5100

COUNTY SOUND RADIO AM
(Guildford, Haslemere, Reigate and Crawley)
Tel: (9293) 519161

GREAT NORTH RADIO
(Tyne & Wear/Teesside)
Tel: 091-496 0377

GREAT YORKSHIRE RADIO
(Yorkshire, Lincolnshire)
Tel: (0742) 852121

LBC NEWSTALK
(London)
Tel: 071-603 2400

LONDON TALKBACK RADIO
(London)
Tel: 071-333 0003

METRO FM
(Tyne & Wear)
Tel: 091-488 3131

MIDLANDS RADIO plc
(BRMB FM, GEM AM, Leicester Sound FM, Mercia FM, Trent FM
(Nottingham), Trent FM (Derby), Xtra AM)
Tel: (0602) 503020

MORAY FIRTH RADIO
(Inverness)
Tel: (0463) 224433

PICCADILLY KEY 103
(Greater Manchester)
Tel: 061-236 9913

THE PULSE
(Bradford, Huddersfield and Halifax)
Tel: (0274) 731521

Q96
(Paisley)
Tel: 041-887 9630

RADIOWAVE
(Blackpool)
Tel: (0253) 304965

RTM
(Thamesmead)
Tel: 081-311 3112

SOUTH WEST SOUND
(Dumfries and Galloway)
Tel: (0387) 50999

RADIO TAVISTOCK
(Tavistock)
Tel: (0752) 227272

THE WORLD'S GREATEST MUSIC STATION
(Peterborough (mid-Anglia region))
Tel: (0733) 34622